Toilets,
Toasters
&Telephones

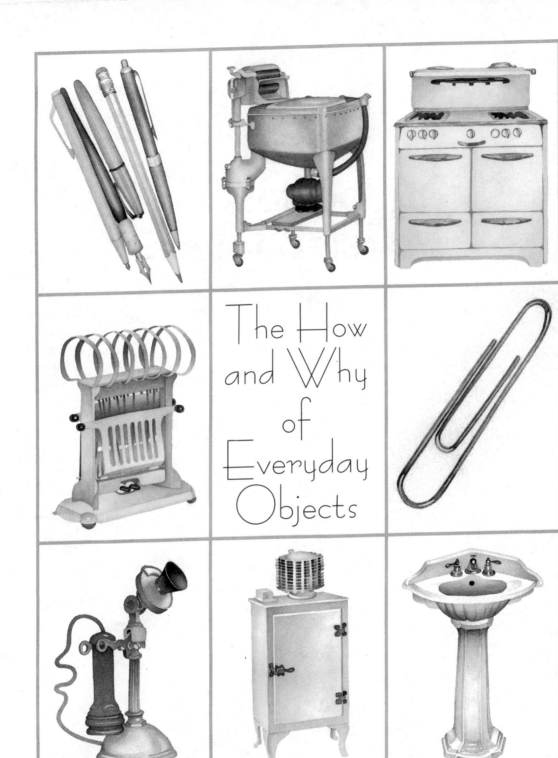

The How
and Why
of
Everyday
Objects

Toilets, Toasters & Telephones

SUSAN GOLDMAN RUBIN

Illustrated with photographs
and with illustrations by

ELSA WARNICK

SCHOLASTIC INC.
New York Toronto London Auckland Sydney
Mexico City New Delhi Hong Kong

To my agent, George M. Nicholson,
and my editor, Linda Zuckerman
—S. G. R.

For Jerry Hart
—E. W.

ISBN 0-439-10492-0

12 11 10 9 8 7 6 5 4 3 2 1   9/9 0 1 2 3 4/0

Printed in the U.S.A.   23

First Scholastic printing, September 1999

The illustrations for this book were done in watercolor
on Lanaquarelle 140 lb. hot-press watercolor paper.
The display type was set in Futura Book.
The text type was set in Stone Serif.
Designed by Lydia D'moch

Cover photograph courtesy of the Warshaw Collection of Business Americana,
Archives Center, National Museum of American History,
Smithsonian Institution.

Permissions acknowledgements appear on pages 117-119, which constitute
a continuation of the copyright page.

Contents

List of Illustrations

Introduction

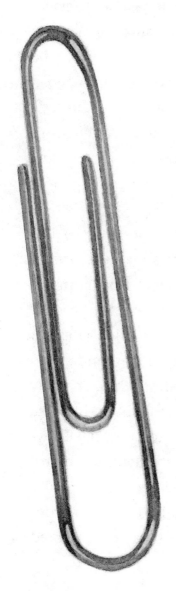

Every day people use toilets, sinks, toothbrushes, clocks, telephones, TVs, refrigerators, ovens, toasters, trash cans, vacuum cleaners, hangers, paper clips, zippers, safety pins, pencils, and pens. These objects are so familiar we take them for granted. But how did these things come to look the way they do? Did they always have the same shape? Were they always the same size and color?

We know that toilets at home may be different from toilets in public places, which may flush with a handle, foot pedal, push button, or even automatically. Why all these changes? Who makes them?

Industrial designers do. They plan the forms of objects that are mass-produced—made by machinery—things as small as pens and toothbrushes or as big as cars and airplanes. Industrial designers work in teams consisting of manufacturers and their production staff: researchers, engineers, toolmakers, and salespeople. They are artists who dream up ideas for new products that are then made by engineers. Their goal is to design things that work easily, can be produced as cheaply as possible, and also look good. When a machine-made thing does its job well—like a pen that is comfortable to hold, writes smoothly, is pleasing to look at, and doesn't leak—it makes life more pleasant. One of the first American industrial designers, Norman Bel Geddes, said that "when a thing is designed right, it looks right."

Sometimes a company hires an industrial designer to improve a product and make it look better. Once a manufacturer of flyswatters came to Henry Dreyfuss, another great pioneer in the field. The manufacturer wanted Dreyfuss to redesign the product to increase sales. While they chatted, Dreyfuss doodled a design. He changed the swatting part from an oblong to a round shape with a bull's-eye and gave it a handle like a riding whip. The new flyswatter looked more like a piece of sports equipment than like hardware. The manufacturer asked what the fee was, but Dreyfuss refused any payment. The company put the design into production and months later Dreyfuss started receiving royalty checks for his work. His new flyswatter had boosted sales from the thousands to millions. It looked so great that people wanted to buy it.

In 1938 the Museum of Modern Art in New York began to recognize what it called "applied art." It held exhibitions featuring furniture and household objects that the museum directors considered efficient and beautiful. And because they believed that things with good form and color don't have to cost more than poorly designed things, in 1941 the museum directors displayed *Useful Objects Under Ten Dollars*. The exhibit included salt and pepper shakers, pliers, an alarm clock, a garden trowel, a pencil with a night-light in its stem, and a key ring and change holder. The point of the show was to help people choose well-designed objects that functioned or did their job properly. The museum saw itself as a kind of teacher that could raise the level of the public's taste. No longer were fine things reserved for a privileged few. Now everyone could enjoy them—if they were able to recognize them. The museum hoped to guide people into acquiring a sense of aesthetics, a way of judging that which is beautiful, honest, and truly of quality.

This book looks at many ordinary household objects to reveal how they were designed and explores the times in which these things were created—for our household objects offer an understanding of history, culture, and changing attitudes in the United States during the twentieth century.

1

A Bathroom
Is a Bathroom

Toilets

Fig. 1.1.

One of the most frequently used objects in the house is the toilet. But what did people use before they had bathrooms? In earliest times people relieved themselves wherever they happened to be—in the woods, a field, or in a running stream of water.

Then, in ancient civilizations, bathrooms were built for rulers and rich people. In the palace at Knossos in Crete, an island near Greece, there was a modern indoor toilet with a wooden seat built around 2000 B.C. A house in the ancient Egyptian city of Tel el Amarna had a toilet seat made of limestone shaped like buttocks (Fig. 1.2).

To the west of Egypt a colony called Carthage was founded in 814 B.C. War broke out between Carthage and Rome. After many years of fighting, Rome finally destroyed Carthage and took over all of North Africa in 146 B.C. The Roman soldiers had public urinals and latrines as well as private bathrooms. At Timgad, in North Africa, archaeologists found a room with twenty-five stone seats, each one separated by the carving of a dolphin. Apparently the ancient Romans enjoyed "going to the bathroom" together.

Back home in Rome, the soldiers had wooden seats along two sides of a trough. The ancient Romans built latrines over running water to carry off wastes to the Tiber River, which ran into the Mediterranean Sea. They developed the art of plumbing and constructed underground sewers. The sewers, like tunnels, also drained excess rainwater so that the streets wouldn't flood. The sewer pipes were made of lead, earthenware, or

Fig. 1.2. An early Egyptian toilet seat dating from roughly 1370 B.C. The split in the seat is similar to the split found in some public toilet seats today.

stone. When the Saxons, Danes, and other invaders conquered Rome, they destroyed or ignored civilized achievements such as plumbing.

In the Middle Ages, from about A.D. 500 to 1500, most people were ignorant of sanitation. Open cesspools bred terrible diseases. Castles had latrines built into niches in the walls. Drains carried the waste down into the moat surrounding the castle. At night ordinary people in the British Isles used chamber pots made of glass and metal. In the morning before they emptied their chamber pots out the window they shouted, *"Gardy-loo!"* (fractured French for *Guardez l'eau!,* "Watch out for water!"). The word *loo,* used in Britain and the United States as a more polite, delicate way of referring to the toilet or bathroom, probably comes from the cry *"Gardy-loo!"* Of course, the streets were a stinking, disgusting mess.

For hundreds of years people in western Europe lived in filthy conditions. Cities including London and Paris grew up without adequate sewers. In London public latrines were built over the Thames and Fleet Rivers. In Paris wastes flowed down gutters and into old sewers clogged with garbage and then into the Seine. People got their drinking water from these rivers.

Some rich people had portable toilets called close-stools or stools of ease. They were shaped like boxes with lids and had carrying handles. Queen Elizabeth I used one covered with red velvet and trimmed in lace until her godson, Sir John Harington, invented a flushing toilet for her in 1596. It was the first flushing toilet! He wrote a book about it with directions for how to build one, but few people did. Then, nearly two hundred years later, Alexander Cummings, a London watchmaker, received a patent for the flushing toilet that is the forerunner of the model used today. Joseph Bramah, an English cabinetmaker, greatly improved it and manufactured thousands of toilets with cast-iron bowls.

But most of London still had no sewers. And the countryside didn't, either. Cesspits collected the wastes. Even the best houses had cesspits in the yard or underneath the living room floor. "Night men" carried away the contents in the dark. At one house the smell was so bad that a plumber was hired to clean out the drain. When he opened the floor, he found fifty rats' nests (along with silver spoons, scissors, and corkscrews). He sent in a cat to get rid of the rats, but the poor creature died, overcome by the experience.

Meanwhile, many people were still using chamber pots. Now they were made of porcelain and so beautifully decorated they were works of art. Some had flowers modeled on the outside or a realistic frog inside. Others were jokey and had portraits of political figures like Napoléon Bonaparte and Benjamin Franklin painted in the center. A popular model featured a large eye with the words *Use me well, and keep me clean, and I'll not tell what I have seen.*

In Britain there were also public privies or outhouses. The word *privy* meant "private" or "withdrawn from public sight." These little buildings had a board inside with holes cut out for seats. Underneath there was a pit or bucket to catch the wastes. Early settlers in the United States built outhouses, too. The inside was often decorated with wallpaper and cut-up sections of newspaper and catalogs. These came in handy for reading as well as wiping.

Towns and cities grew up without sewers or septic systems. Across the ocean in Britain, sanitary conditions remained equally bad. Then a disease called cholera swept across Europe from Asia and hit London and Paris in 1832. Millions died. People finally began to realize that contaminated water caused and spread disease. Parisians rioted and Emperor Napoléon III had old sewers cleaned and new ones built. Reformers in Britain also demanded improvements. The government passed laws requiring houses to have some kind of flushing toilet or privy.

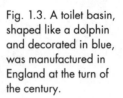

Fig. 1.3. A toilet basin, shaped like a dolphin and decorated in blue, was manufactured in England at the turn of the century.

By the 1880s Britain had good sewers and led the world in the production of indoor "water closets," or toilets. Thomas Crapper, a plumber, developed a type of flushing toilet in 1872 that carried his name. He perfected the cistern—the tank that holds the water for flushing. And he made flushing quieter. Women at the turn of the century, sensitive to bodily noises, wanted a "really silent toilet." Crapper did such fine work that he became the royal plumber and installed more than thirty toilets in Sandringham Castle for Queen Victoria's son Edward, Prince of Wales. A book written about Crapper was called *Flushed with Pride.* The author wrote, "There is no question that Crapper's heart was in the toilet."

The Victorians regarded the toilet as a status symbol. Basins were made of fine glazed earthenware and hand painted with tulips, roses, chrysanthemums, and daisies. Some were sculpted as lions and swans holding the basins on their backs.

One of the first Americans to have an indoor toilet was the poet Henry Wadsworth Longfellow. Besides poetry, Longfellow was interested in teaching, technology, health, and traveling. When he visited Europe, he discovered indoor plumbing. Back home at Craigie House in Cambridge, Massachusetts, he installed a toilet in the basement and tore down his outside privy. In those days, the 1840s, most people were scared by indoor bathrooms and thought they would spread disease. Longfellow was proud of his up-to-date home improvements (including a shower in his dressing room) and showed off his house to the many guests who gathered there. Because he was an extremely popular American poet, a celebrity, he influenced people's opinions about a great number of things, including household arrangements. Longfellow inspired other Americans to have bathrooms and by 1860, when indoor plumbing became available, many wealthy homes had flush toilets.

These early models were imported from England. The tanks had pull-chains and were mounted high on the wall above the bowls (Fig. 1.1). The porcelain basins were ornamented with dolphins, an old favorite from Roman times. But the dolphins' ornate fins and faces were too hard to keep clean (Fig. 1.3). So the Standard Sanitary Manufacturing Company offered a simpler toilet with a plain bowl. From 1910 to the 1920s, the elevated water tank was gradually lowered and placed closer to the bowl until tank and bowl finally became one unit.

In the early part of the twentieth century, people became more concerned with cleanliness. They worried about dirt and germs because they had learned that germs carry disease. White was the preferred color for bathrooms because it looked sanitary. The bathroom was supposed to be a kind of "hospital in the home."

But starting in the late 1920s, people wanted their bathrooms to be beautiful as well as clean. White seemed dull. Magazine ads encouraged people to decorate their bathrooms as artful expressions of their personalities. Manufacturers introduced colors in toilets, bathtubs, and sinks. First there were pastels—pink, yellow, and green—then deeper shades, even black. As companies competed for customers, they had to come up with better-looking products. They hired industrial designers.

Industrial design began as a profession in the late 1920s as Americans demanded more beautiful machine-made products for their homes. The artists and designers who made these things were inspired by the machines themselves. They liked the looks of ball bearings, springs, and propellers, and they saw beauty in simple geometric shapes. Machinery also symbolized power and progress. When the Great Depression hit in 1929, industrial designers were hired to remodel old products to make them cheaper yet attractive so that the public would buy them and keep manufacturers in business. For example, industrial designers restyled toasters, stoves, pots, pans, irons, radios, and hundreds of other items. An article in *Fortune* magazine in 1934 told about the designers' work and showed before-and-after photographs of toasters and stoves. The point of the article was that more attractive appliances sold better, proving that "beauty did, indeed, pay."

"The goal of design is sales," said Harold Van Doren, one of the first American industrial designers. (His "penny-in-the-slot" public weighing scale, shaped like a skyscraper, was said to have increased sales by 900 percent!) This made more jobs for people who needed work in hard times.

In the 1930s, the Crane Company hired Henry Dreyfuss to design a new line of matching bathroom fixtures. Dreyfuss approached the problem using a system of human engineering called ergonomics, which means considering how people relate to machine-made tools and equipment. He designed products that not only looked good but were comfortable, safe, and easy to use. The motto in his office was: "We bear in mind that the object we are working on is going to be ridden in, sat upon, looked at, talked into, activated, operated, or in some other way used by people." Dreyfuss wanted to create objects—in this case toilets, sinks, and tubs—that would fit people. "The most efficient machine," he said, "is the one that is built around a person."

Dreyfuss found out what the Crane Company wanted and imagined what the customer would like. "The designer does the dreaming," he said. "The engineer makes the dreams come true." Back in his office, he made hundreds of sketches. (Dreyfuss always carried small sharp pencils in his pockets. He developed a knack for drawing upside down, so that at a meeting the person he was talking to on the other side of the table could easily see what he was explaining.)

In designing the Neuvogue toilet, for instance, Dreyfuss

considered dimensions. How high off the floor should the toilet be? Where should the handle be placed for flushing? How wide a toilet seat would fit any person? What would be the best shape?

Dreyfuss knew that there were many ways to approach a design problem. His method involved extensive research. He had collected measurements and dimensions for the average man, woman, and child, so that any apparatus would be sure to fit any size person. (Dreyfuss applied his philosophy to everything from bathroom fixtures to farm machinery. For example, Deere & Company hired him to replace a wide tractor seat. He was amused to learn how the old seat had been designed. The engineers in the factory, wanting to create a seat that would fit everyone, simply took the man with the biggest behind and sat him in plaster.)

Dreyfuss's method for designing the wide tractor seat, as well as the Neuvogue toilet seat, was more scientific. Research showed that a squatting position was more natural and comfortable for emptying the bowels, so Dreyfuss invented a seat that sloped backward.

Next he made a three-dimensional scale model. Dreyfuss said, "As soon as possible, we get a form into clay and actually do our designing in this pliable material." Later models were developed in plaster, wood, or plastic. Finally a full-size working model was presented to the client, the Crane Company. Dreyfuss listened to suggestions and kept improving the product. After many months the new toilet was finished and displayed in showrooms and catalogs. Unfortunately, the toilet seat, though functionally correct, failed to attract customers and was discontinued. Perhaps it was just too unusual. Over the years Dreyfuss designed various kinds of toilets in addition to the Neuvogue. One model, named the Walsan Closet, fastened to the wall. (Frank Lloyd Wright, the architect, claimed to have invented the first wall-hung toilet in 1904 for his Larkin Building in Buffalo, New York. He designed this type of toilet to make mopping a bathroom floor quicker and easier. Yet, Thomas Crapper in England had developed and marketed a wall-hung toilet in 1888 for prisons and mental institutions, where floors had to be cleaned often. Perhaps Wright didn't know about Crapper's toilet.)

Many architects as well as industrial designers were interested in modernizing the bathroom. R. Buckminster Fuller, an inventor, came up with the idea of a prefabricated bathroom that could be installed in any living space cheaply and easily. All the parts— toilet, tub, sink, and shower—were stamped out of a continuous piece of glass-reinforced plastic. Fuller received a patent for his design in 1940, but it didn't catch on in the United States. Customers didn't like bathroom fixtures made of plastic. They preferred china and porcelain. And workers in the construction industry objected to prefabrication. But Fuller's bathroom was successfully mass-produced in Germany. The fiberglass showers in use now in apartments, houses, and motels are an outgrowth of his idea.

Today's designers are combining old styles with new plumbing. A contemporary "1930s toilet," for example, looks like a fixture from that period. Another model, decorated with garlands of blue

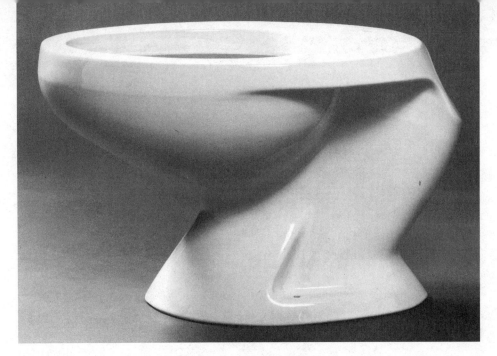

Fig. 1.4. A toilet designed in 1953 by Gio Ponti, an Italian designer, architect, professor, and writer. It won a gold medal for good design in Milan, Italy.

flowers, resembles a Victorian water closet. People are asking for heated toilet seats and for toilets that flush silently.

Industrial designers, aware of environmental issues, are thinking up ways for toilets to use less water. One company produces toilets that recycle wastewater from the sink into the tank. Another company manufactures an ultra low flush model that uses only 1.6 gallons of water, compared to older tanks that used from 2.75 to 4 gallons. Yet a toilet crisis occurred in 1996, when thousands of the low flush toilets backed up and overflowed. The toilets lacked flushing power because they had so little water; even a wadded-up tissue couldn't go down in one flush. People went to junkyards and garage sales and bought the old models that flushed better.

Sinks

Fig. 1.5.

How many times a day do people wash their hands? Dozens. First thing in the morning, before meals, after using the bathroom . . . Ancient Egyptian and Greek pictures show men and women washing with water poured from jugs. People in many parts of the world still wash this way. Probably millions more people use water poured from jugs than use sinks with plumbing. Before plumbing, there were no "rooms" for washing. "Sinks" were portable in the form of bowls or pitchers of water and so could be brought to the table, like finger bowls today.

In the twelfth and thirteenth centuries, western Europeans ate with their fingers and washed their hands before and after dinner. Sometimes they washed each other's fingers for fun. At grand parties a trumpet sounded, signaling that it was time to wash. Then a young page boy knelt before each guest and held out a full basin of water (often scented with rose petals), an empty basin, and a towel. Soap was not brought to the table. Princes and dukes owned fancy sets of jugs and basins made of gold and silver.

In the bedrooms of that time, there were portable washstands. Medieval books about good manners instructed people to wash their hands, face, and teeth every morning but *not* to take a bath.

The French word for *washstand* was *lavabo*. It came from the phrase *donner à laver,* which means "to offer a wash." The English word became *lavatory.* In the eighteenth century, lavatories stood on three dainty legs. Then in England the lavatories became pieces of furniture. Cabinetmakers included folding

shelves and drawers and a hidden chamber pot "for the acciden-
tal occasions of the night."

By 1830 lavatories looked like marble-topped tables with
shelves below. A jug held at least a gallon of cold water. In well-to-
do homes maids ran up and down the stairs, filling and emptying
the jugs and basins.

When running water became available in England, after
1870, the lavatory became a permanent fixture. Sometimes it
was still in the bedroom, but often it had a room of its own—the
bathroom.

As manufacturing techniques improved, sinks were mass-
produced. From the 1880s to the 1940s, sinks were either wall
mounted or supported by a pedestal (Fig. 1.5). A better clay
material called vitreous china was developed for sinks. It didn't
absorb water and it had a gleaming surface that looked clean.
Vitreous china was used for all the fixtures in the bathroom.

Twentieth-century industrial designers thought of the bathroom as one package. Sinks or "lavatories" (as they were called
by dealers and designers in the 1930s and 1940s because the
word sounded fancier) matched toilets and bathtubs. Sinks came
in different shapes—square, rectangular, oval, and round. Some
had towel bars attached to the side and mirrors and soap dishes,
just like old-fashioned lavatories.

George Sakier, a New York engineer who had studied art in
Paris, worked as a staff designer for the American Radiator &
Standard Sanitary Corporation in the United States. One of his
most famous designs was a prefabricated floor-to-ceiling unit

consisting of washbasin, cabinet, and mirror framed by fluorescent lights (Fig. 1.6). The sink was a simple rectangle set on tubular chrome legs. The fittings or knobs for the faucets were shaped like balls and made of unbreakable china. Harold Van Doren praised the fittings as "the last word in simplicity for mass production" and showed a close-up picture of the faucets in his book *Industrial Design*. Sakier's lavatory was included in the New York Museum of Modern Art exhibition *Machine Art*. Objects were chosen for this exhibit to prove that appearance was as important as usefulness.

Sakier's lavatory showed the beauty of good machine art. First of all, it was visually pleasing. The lavatory was well proportioned—the parts balanced one another. The vertical shape of the entire unit repeated in

Fig. 1.6. Lavatory panel of the Arco Panel Unit System, equipped with special tubular fittings, designed by George Sakier in 1934 for the Accessories Co., Inc., Division of American Radiator Company

the shelves, mirror, niches for fluorescent lights, and spaces formed by the chrome legs supporting the basin. The repetition of the straight lines created a rhythm that is pleasing to the eye. The curved tubular water spout echoed the shape of the chrome legs. The unadorned surfaces were easy to clean. And built-in shelves provided compact storage areas. Last but not least, the lavatory worked! Hot and cold water could be adjusted to the right temperature in the single spout.

Dreyfuss also wanted to update the bathroom and create forms that were easy to use and keep clean. Like Sakier, he believed that every detail mattered, right down to the faucets and handles. What shapes would be easiest to grasp and turn with wet hands—a single handle or one with four knobs that fit between the thumb and fingers? Which would be better—one spout or two? Dreyfuss experimented with separate handles for hot and cold water, and single handles. They were oblong or round in shape and made of metal or Lucite.

Sometimes he failed. Just after World War II, Dreyfuss designed a sink handle made of gray plastic. "It seemed a good idea at the time," he said, because metal was still scarce and chrome was particularly hard to get. But customers didn't like the ugly gray color, which reminded them of war and wartime materials.

Other new ideas flopped dismally. In the mid-1930s the Kohler Company introduced a "dental lavatory," a small sink just for brushing teeth. American Standard offered one, too, and called it the Denlava. But people didn't buy those, either.

Gio Ponti, who designed a stunning toilet in 1953 (Fig. 1.4), also created a matching sink the same year. He didn't give the basin the usual geometric shape. Instead, his basin was shaped at an angle, like the arms of a person washing. Ponti called this a "true form" because it grew from its function. His sink and matching toilet are so much like pieces of sculpture that they are part of the collection of the Philadelphia Museum of Art. Ponti's fixtures were included in an exhibit in 1983 called *Design Since 1945*. The Decorative Arts Department of this museum, like others in the United States, wanted to show the public beautiful household objects and inspire people to start thinking about the shapes of everyday things. What really looks good? And, like other museums, the Philadelphia Museum of Art wanted to preserve pieces of historical significance. Although Ponti's bathroom fixtures sold well and stayed in production for twenty-five years, there weren't many around after 1975. The curators at the museum kept his sink and toilet in their collection for future generations to see and appreciate.

Despite Ponti's efforts to reshape sinks, many of today's designs copy old styles. Some sinks are even built into washstands that look exactly like nineteenth-century English lavatories. Maybe some people aren't ready for modern design, no matter how beautiful it is. They're nostalgic—that is, they like things that remind them of a much earlier era. Henry Dreyfuss understood this. He said, "People will more readily accept something new . . . if they recognize in it something out of the past." When he created any new form, he tried to include a detail or pattern from something old and familiar.

Bathtubs

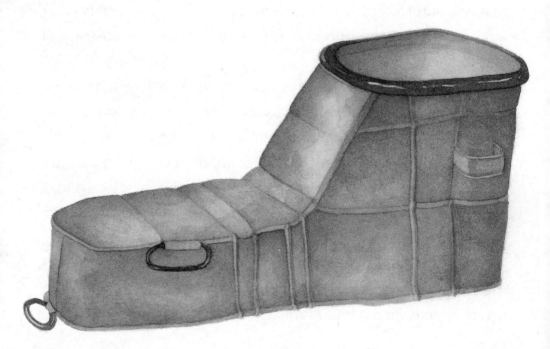

Fig. 1.7.

The shape of the bathtub has changed surprisingly little through the years. That's understandable, though, because the human body hasn't changed—and tubs fit people. The earliest bathtub was found in the bathroom in the palace of King Minos at Knossos. The palace dates back to 2000 B.C. The tub was made of clay and was filled and emptied by hand. The outside was painted with a pattern of reeds. Other ancient civilizations—the Greeks, Romans, Egyptians, Chinese, and Japanese—took baths for recreation or hygiene, sometimes as often as twice a day. Bathing was the most important social activity for the Romans, who built huge public bathhouses that could hold sixteen hundred people at a time.

But early Christians in Europe disapproved of bathing. They thought it was sinful and unhealthful, and acceptable only as a cure for sickness. Saint Agnes, a follower of Francis of Assisi, died at age thirteen without ever having washed.

In medieval times, people bathed occasionally. Illustrated manuscripts and woodcuts show rich families and their friends taking a bath together in a big round tub while musicians played for them (Fig. 1.8). In those days, when an entire household slept in one room, people didn't think about privacy.

In the fifteenth century, public baths became popular and were called stews. A street in London had so many bathhouses it was named Stew Lane. Boys ran through the streets announcing when the water was hot. Stews soon disappeared, however, because people were frightened by the spread of plagues and other infections. They believed disease was caused by people

Fig. 1.8. *The Children's Bath* (portion of the engraving) by Israhel van Meckenem, German 1440/1450–1503

soaking together. Historians refer to the next two centuries as the "dirty days" because people didn't bathe. A Frenchman in 1655 wrote, "The bath destroys the body."

In the eighteenth century, doctors knew more about cleanliness and urged people to wash. Bathtubs then were big wooden boxes with padded backs and armrests, lined with lead or copper. People entertained and had their portraits painted while they were taking a bath.

Next there were portable bathtubs in different shapes and sizes. Usually they were made of copper and, sometimes, tin. Benjamin Franklin brought a copper slipper bath back from France. It was shaped like a short boot (Fig. 1.7). When he sat in it, only his head and shoulders stuck out. Jean-Paul Marat, a leader in the French Revolution, spent hours in his slipper bath. One evening, while taking a bath and writing an article, he was stabbed to death by a political enemy, Charlotte Corday. (The artist Jacques-Louis David painted a picture of the murder scene, and it hangs in the Musée Royaux des Beaux-Arts in Brussels.)

In the nineteenth century, bathtubs began to look more like those used today. They were made of cast metal and had legs with feet shaped like paws or claws (Fig. 1.9). The British started producing solid porcelain tubs, but they were too heavy to ship to America.

At that time most Americans didn't enjoy bathing, anyway. Like the French two hundred years earlier, they believed water weakened a healthy person. However, some Native Americans viewed bathing differently. Tribes such as the Chumash, Shawnee, and Klamath River Indians built sweat houses, or sweat lodges, that had fire pits inside. Certain members of the tribe (men, women, or children, according to the rules) used the sweat houses not only for getting clean but for purification and healing ceremonies. After working up a sweat by the fire, they jumped into a nearby stream to cool off.

The Aztecs in Mexico bathed frequently in rivers and streams. Indoors, they had a kind of sauna or steam bath for cleaning themselves, relaxing, treating certain diseases, and performing rituals.

Gradually the American settlers' attitudes changed. Pioneers going west took along portable steam baths. "Steam doctors" traveled around the country recommending "Cold . . . Warm, Hot, Vapour, Gas & Mud Baths."

Early Americans placed their tubs in the kitchen near the stove where the teakettle was heating. On Saturday nights the grown-ups and children took turns bathing. The oldest bathed first. By the time the youngest got into the tub, the water was gray. When running water became available, bathrooms became separate rooms. Tubs were installed as permanent fixtures.

It was hard to clean underneath the low claw-foot tubs. Soon the feet disappeared. As early as 1911, the Kohler Company introduced a built-in bathtub set flat on the floor. The standard size became five feet long. Some people didn't fit.

President William Howard Taft, our largest president, was six feet tall and weighed more than three hundred pounds. He was called Big Bill. When he moved into the White House in 1909, a special bathtub had to be installed for him. Newspaper pictures showed four big workmen sitting in the oversized tub.

Back then the shower was usually a separate fixture, placed next to the bathtub. It was shaped like a cylinder, with round metal bars and enclosed by a curtain. Taking a shower was considered a type of washing mainly for men and was nicknamed the "morning bracer" or the "rain bath." (An earlier "rain bath," in the nineteenth century, had been a medical treatment. A

Fig. 1.9. A nursemaid dries off her charge, who's just had a bath in this claw-footed tub, circa 1910.

patient stood in a pit with a nozzle overhead. Then a doctor pulled a cord, releasing a torrent of water. One observer wrote, "It is no rare thing to see a subject who at this first shower betrays actual terror, shouts, struggles, runs away, experiences frightening suffocation and palpitation; and it is not rare to hear him say, after a few moments, 'So that's all it is.'")

In 1912 the Standard Sanitary Manufacturing Company

offered a combined built-in bathtub and shower. It quickly became a standard item. By the 1920s showering was popular with women, too.

Glass shower doors became an option in the 1940s. People began to wonder which was better—a bath or a shower? Ogden Nash wrote a poem about it:

> *Some people are do-it-some-other-timers and other*
> *people are do-it-nowers,*
> *And that is why manufacturers keep on manufacturing*
> *both bathtubs and showers,*
> *Because some bathers prefer to recline*
> *On the cornerstone of their spine,*
> *While others, who about their comfort are less particular,*
> *Bathe perpendicular.*

For people who enjoyed taking a bath, designers came up with new features. Jacuzzi offered a whirlpool bath with jets that shot out powerful streams of bubbles. Foam headrests and built-in armrests made soaking more comfortable. Tubs became available in larger sizes. Despite the new frills, many people still prefer a tub that looks old-fashioned.

Hot tubs became popular in the late 1970s. The first ones were made from old wine barrels. In warm weather, families and friends bathed together outdoors in the wooden tubs, just as they had done in medieval times. As the trend caught on, manufacturers made hot tubs from redwood, cedar, and teak.

Sometimes the wood rotted, so portable tubs called spas were made, fiberglass shells nestling in wooden cases. Some people put hot tubs on the roofs of their homes, so that at night they could gaze at the stars while they sat and soaked.

Industrial designers keep trying to understand what people want in a modern bathroom. Surveys show that people ask for improvements such as a separate tub for washing pets. Should the bathroom be luxurious or simply clean and practical? Nowadays, it's both.

2
What's Cooking?

Stoves

Fig. 2.1.

When fire was discovered, it was first used for heating, then for cooking. People realized that meat tasted better when it was cooked. The earliest method of cooking was probably a rotisserie made from two Y-shaped twigs that held a spit. Cooking pits have been found in houses dating back to the Stone Age. They were pits dug in the floor in the center of the room and lined with stone. Some of them had a low stone platform on which to rest a pot. A hole was cut in the roof of the house to let out the smoke.

Ancient Greeks and Romans built big houses but made the kitchen a separate building. Roman slaves did all the cooking on a charcoal fire in a fireplace. In the ruins of the ancient city of Pompeii, in Italy, fireplaces have been found with kettles still hanging in place. One oven even contained the loaves of bread that were baking when Mount Vesuvius erupted in the year A.D. 79!

During the Middle Ages, peasants cooked outdoors or in hearths in their cottages. Castles and monasteries had huge kitchens, where meals were prepared for hundreds of people at a time. One fireplace was big enough for roasting a whole ox and a turnspit of birds. A small boy, also called a turnspit, turned the spit by hand to roast the meat evenly. He made sure the roast was "done to a turn." Later, dogs harnessed to a treadmill attached to the spit did the same job (Fig. 2.2). According to one writer, geese were even better turnspits, "for they will bear their Labour longer, so that if there be need they will continue their Labour 12 Hours."

Cooking scenes in tapestries, woodcuts, and manuscripts show that Europeans continued to spit-roast and grill their meat

31

Fig. 2.2. This late-eighteenth-century kitchen in South Wales had a dog-driven spit. The dog (top center) runs in a hollow wheel connected by chains to a spit in the fireplace that slowly turns the meat. Short-legged dogs were especially trained for this purpose. This drawing is based on a painting by Thomas Rowlandson.

through the sixteenth century. In those days, kitchens were often divided into separate rooms for different purposes. There were bakehouses, dairies, pantries, smokehouses, and sometimes a special room for preparing medicines from herbs.

When the first colonists came to America, they lived in simple one-room cabins. As they became more prosperous, they built grand houses in what is now called the Colonial style. The kitchens were in separate buildings to prevent heat and odors from coming into the main house. At George Washington's estate, Mount Vernon, in Virginia, the kitchen was next to the big house.

New inventions in the eighteenth century made cooking easier. At Mount Vernon a device was connected to a mechanical fan that turned the spit in the fireplace. This is how it worked: The smoke from a roaring fire rotated the fan, which caused the spit to turn. Another tool was a clockwork "spit-jack," wound up with a key, so that boys, dogs, and geese no longer had to do the job.

In 1780 Thomas Robinson, an Englishman, took out a patent for the first kitchen range. He probably designed it himself, as did many early inventors. It had a cast-iron oven on one side and a boiler for heating water on the other. Although it wasn't beautiful, it worked! Two decades later, in 1802, George Bodley, an ironfounder, patented a closed-top cooking range that was the prototype of today's stoves. The closed range was popular although it burned large amounts of coal and was extremely hot, dirty, and difficult to use.

In America, during the early 1800s, people used a kind of range called a kitchener. It, too, burned coal and created a great deal of soot and smoke. Even though kitcheners were black, they had to be brushed clean every day. And there was no way yet to control the temperature. In a Vermont cookbook the author suggested:

For pies, cakes, and white bread the heat of the oven should be such that you can hold your hand and arm [in the oven] while you count 40; for brown bread, meats, beans, Indian puddings and pumpkin pies, it should be hotter, so that you can only hold it in while you count 20.

The biggest improvement came with the introduction of gas stoves in the middle of the nineteenth century. Technology led to this improvement. A new fuel had become available—coal gas. At first it was used for lighting factories, public buildings, and streets. Then, when electricity became available, gas companies competed and laid pipes to carry gas into houses. Gas stoves were cleaner and easier to use, and the heat could be easily adjusted. In the beginning, housewives distrusted this new method of cooking. They thought they'd be poisoned or blown up. A famous chef in London installed gas stoves in the kitchens of his club and gave demonstrations, but people still weren't convinced.

A woman in Northampton, England, bought a gas cooker and proudly showed it to her husband. He was horrified and said he'd never eat anything cooked on it. She wanted to keep it. So she tricked him by cooking his dinner in the gas stove, then transferring it to the open fire minutes before he came home from work. He never found out.

By the end of the nineteenth century, gas stoves were finally accepted. At that time electricity became available for home use. Americans liked electric cooking. They wanted kitchen work to be automatic. An article in *Good Housekeeping* magazine in 1930 asked readers, "How many times have you wished you could push a button and find your meals deliciously prepared and served, and then as easily cleared away by the snap of a switch?"

Manufacturers of gas stoves competed with companies that made electric ones. Both types looked the same. They stood on slender curved legs. The basic design was split-level, with ovens on one side, a cooktop on the other, and a storage area beneath. The designers of these early stoves remained anonymous. The manufacturers who hired them preferred to keep it that way. They may have worried that if the designers became well known, they would demand more money. In 1923 thermostats were invented. Cooks could then control temperatures without sticking their arms inside the oven.

In the 1930s manufacturers needed to make their products more appealing so that people would buy them. They hired artists who applied their skills and talents to designing everyday objects. These first industrial designers quickly gained recognition and did ask for higher fees—but their designs also greatly increased their employers' profits. Well-designed products looked better, worked better, and sold better.

Norman Bel Geddes designed the Oriole stove for the Standard Gas Equipment Corporation, and it became a classic (Fig. 2.3). Bel Geddes, a high school dropout, started his career in New York City as a theater set designer. He also dressed department store windows in startling, original ways that caught people's attention. But he was best known for designing ships, cars, and a rotating restaurant on top of a tower. For the Oriole stove he created one simple boxy unit in white, the most "sanitary"-looking color. It had no legs, so it was not necessary to clean beneath it. Bel Geddes described his stove as "a plain out-and-out cooking machine with no trick features, no gadgets, no decoration to dress it up. It does all that any other stove will do as

Fig. 2.3. Standard Gas Equipment, model stove, designed by Norman Bel Geddes, 1933

simply and as well, and is the easiest stove to use and keep clean on the market to-day."

The Oriole stove was a huge success. Other companies copied it. But during World War II, production of all kitchen appliances slowed down. Bel Geddes, Dreyfuss, and other major industrial designers put their efforts into war work.

After the war there was a boom in manufacturing. Designers came up with many new ideas. One trend in the kitchen was toward continuous counters instead of appliances that stood separately with big spaces in between. For example, the sink, cabinets, and stove were now exactly the same height and depth, forming one uninterrupted unit. (The height was meant to be convenient for the average-sized woman.) Appliances were flush against cabinets. Instead of standing by itself, the stove was sometimes tucked between two cabinets or alongside the sink. The point was to plan the kitchen like a workshop, so that a woman could prepare food, cook, and clean up more efficiently, taking fewer steps.

One company offered disconnected ovens and stove tops that could be placed in different parts of the kitchen. Ovens were built into the walls, with the controls at eye level. Cabinets were finished in the same material and their color harmonized with that of the appliances. Stoves and ovens that had been produced only in white now came in turquoise, copper, avocado, and gold.

Today's stoves come in even more colors—including burgundy red, forest green, blue, and old-fashioned black. Some fancy models have charcoal grills for barbecuing indoors and built-in griddles. One deluxe electric oven features an automatic rotisserie.

A new way of cooking food faster came with the invention of the microwave oven by Dr. Percy L. Spencer, an engineer at the Raytheon Company. In 1945 he was working on radar equipment for use in World War II. As Dr. Spencer stood in front of a microwave tube, he noticed that the chocolate bar in his pocket had melted, but his jacket remained cool and unscorched. The microwaves had stimulated water molecules in the chocolate and caused those molecules to vibrate, which then generated heat that melted the candy. This led Dr. Spencer to believe that microwaves could be used to cook food quickly from the inside out. The story goes that Dr. Spencer and other engineers at Raytheon experimented with different foods. Once they tried to cook an egg. When they leaned over the microwave oven and opened the door, the egg exploded in their faces. They had better luck with popcorn and potatoes.

After Dr. Spencer made his discovery, he worked with technicians and built the first microwave oven. Unfortunately it weighed 750 pounds, stood more than five feet tall, and cost $3,000. It could only be used in large institutions. Then Raytheon tried to develop a microwave oven for home use that would be small enough to fit on a counter. In 1965 Raytheon acquired the Amana company and started working with designers. In 1967 the first successful countertop model, known as the Amana Radarange, was introduced. It sold for $495. Many innovations followed.

Despite all the hoopla, people remained suspicious of the new appliance. They thought the rays would hurt them. Amana did a whistle-stop tour of the suburbs of Chicago. At each stop company representatives brought housewives on board the train and demonstrated that the oven couldn't operate unless the door was fully closed and sealed. Gradually people were won over. Today microwave ovens are found in more than 90 percent of homes in the United States. Some microwave ovens have a button marked POPCORN. One push of the button, and the machine "knows" exactly how long it takes to pop a bag of corn.

Toasters

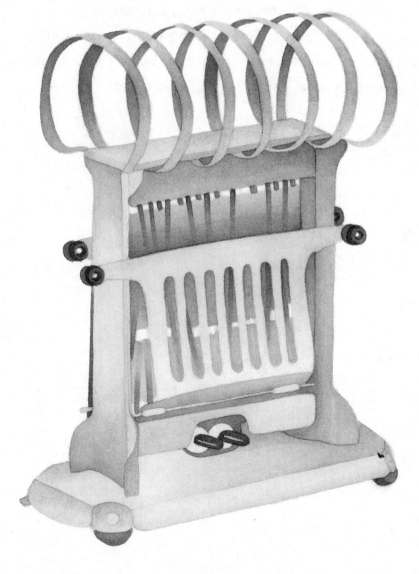

Fig. 2.4.

For hundreds of years people have enjoyed eating toast. The very word *toasty* suggests warmth and comfort. In the Middle Ages enormous fires in the center of the room were surrounded by browning forks on revolving hooks. Eighteenth-century English people made toast in their fireplaces with a rack called the hanging griller. Another tool was the salamander, a metal disk with a long handle that was put into the fire until it was hot, then held close to a slice of bread. (Sometimes people simply used long-handled forks.) In 1791 Thomas Gilray drew caricatures of the king and queen making a midnight snack in front of the fire. The king, in a bathrobe and nightcap, toasts muffins and boils a kettle for tea.

People loved the smell and taste of crisp toast. But they wanted a tool that would make toast more quickly and easily. The first successful electric toaster was manufactured by General Electric in 1909. Called the D-12, it consisted of a wire rack and heating element attached to a porcelain base (one model came decorated with flowers) and toasted one side of bread at a time. When the toast was done, the plug had to be pulled immediately or the toast burned. When companies got serious about toast, the "toaster wars" began.

Newfangled toasters had doors—some were solid, while others had slots or pretty perforated designs. Universal made one model with porcelain knobs (cooler to the touch) on the doors and another with a toast-warming rack that sat on the top like a crown (Fig. 2.4). Westinghouse put out the tin Turnover Toaster. Opening its doors turned the toast! Hotpoint's model tilted the toast out when it was done. Coleman's toaster had drawers that slid out.

Manufacturers next offered "combo" toasters that cooked breakfast right at the table instead of on the stove. Armstrong Electric introduced the Perc-O-Toaster, which could make coffee and toast, and even had a waffle attachment. Hotpoint's El Grillo (an early toaster-stove, a forerunner of the toaster-oven) could poach eggs and fry bacon! But there was still no way to regulate toasting time. People guessed when the toast was done (or peeked) and picked it up by hand.

One man, Charles Strite, got sick and tired of burnt toast (and burnt fingers) and invented an automatic one-slice pop-up toaster in 1919. He concealed the wires in a metal box to improve the appearance of the appliance and make toasting safer. However, it was used only in restaurants. When toaster prices dropped and sliced bread was introduced by Wonder in 1930, sales of toasters for home use skyrocketed.

The Waters Genter Company, which soon became the McGraw Electric Company, introduced the first automatic pop-up toaster for the home in 1926. They called it the Toastmaster. In 1938 the company hired Jean Otis Reinecke to redesign it and cut the cost of manufacturing. Reinecke, an Illinois farmer turned artist, started out as a sign painter. Eventually he went into industrial design and created the Scotch tape dispenser, among many other things. His Toastmaster is considered the most popular electrical appliance ever produced (Fig. 2.5).

Reinecke's goal in redesigning the Toastmaster was to make a product that worked safely, efficiently, and sold well. He didn't care about what it looked like. The three-loop design he created for each side of the toaster served a purpose. It took attention away from any scratches or dings on the chrome surface. There was a temperature control to make toast light, medium, or dark. The toaster toasted bread more quickly than any of its competitors.

Speed mattered. In appearance the Toastmaster perfectly represented American design of that period: It was streamlined. That meant it had a sleek, simple shape, shiny chrome, rounded corners, and horizontal lines suggesting fast cars, trains, and planes. The Department of Industrial Design at the Museum of Modern Art in New York hated Reinecke's toaster and said in its *Bulletin* that the toaster was "streamlined as if it were intended to hurtle through the air at 200 miles an hour (an unhappy use for

Fig. 2.5. Jean Reinecke's Toastmaster toaster, 1943

a breakfast-table utensil)." The *Bulletin* also noted, "This object has never been exhibited by the Museum."

Despite the museum's criticism, many people loved the toaster and bought it. Although today's toasters feature improvements such as four or six slots, each wide enough to hold half a bagel, warming racks for heating croissants, and slide-out crumb trays to make cleaning easier, the classics are still favorites. Reinecke's toaster has recently shown up on greeting cards, stickers, and magnets. Why is it so appealing?

The chrome pop-up toaster was a lovable object—cheerful, dependable, a steady worker. It even starred in the animated movie *The Brave Little Toaster,* based on a children's book. The story told of household appliances designed in the 1940s that no longer felt needed. With the toaster as their leader, they set out to find their owner in hopes that he would still want them.

An issue raised by the story was planned obsolescence— the practice of restyling products every year so that people would throw out perfectly good ones and buy new versions to feel up-to-date. "Is it necessary to redesign quite so often?" asked Van Doren in 1940. He and other industrial designers, including Dreyfuss and Reinecke, tried their best to make products that would last. But new materials and methods of production came along, requiring change. And some manufacturers continued to use planned obsolescence to sell everything from toasters and cars to refrigerators.

Refrigerators

Fig. 2.6.

Before refrigerators were invented, people used ice and snow to keep their food from spoiling. In ancient times before 1000 B.C., the Chinese stored ice and snow in their cellars. Around 500 B.C. the Egyptians and Indians made ice on cold nights by setting water out in earthenware pots and keeping the pots wet. The Roman emperor Nero ordered servants to bring him ice and snow from the Italian Alps.

Through the centuries most people preserved their meat and fish in warm weather by salting, smoking, or pickling it. In medieval times the food was often perfumed. Flowers and spices masked the smell of rancid meat. In London if any butcher knowingly sold bad meat he was punished by having it burnt in front of his nose while he stood locked up in the pillory, unable to move his head.

In the 1700s in England, kitchen servants collected ice in the winter and put it into icehouses, where the sheets of ice were packed in salt, wrapped in strips of flannel, and stored underground to keep them frozen till summer. Americans in those days used ice, too. Thomas Jefferson had an icehouse beneath the terrace of his home, Monticello.

Natural ice refrigeration became a business in America during the 1800s. Machines cut ice cubes and blocks of ice from frozen lakes. The ice was kept in windowless shacks and shipped in pine sawdust, which insulated it. Many homes by then had icehouses like Jefferson's.

The first icebox was exactly that—a wooden box. It was

invented by Thomas Moore, a farmer from Maryland. He called his invention a refrigerator, put it into his wagon, and carried milk and butter in it to the market. For the first time an ice container was movable. Customers were so delighted with the freshness of his dairy products that they were willing to pay him twice as much as the going rate.

At about the same time, Jacob Perkins, an American living in England, received a patent for the first refrigeration machine. It had a hand-turned compressor that evaporated fluid ether to cool down the air inside the box. The story goes that one summer evening Perkins's helpers were working with his refrigerator when it produced ice for the first time. They were so excited that they wrapped up the ice in a blanket and rushed across London in a horse-drawn cab to show it to Perkins at his home. The inventor demonstrated his refrigerator throughout London, but the English wouldn't buy it. They thought anyone making artificial ice was probably in cahoots with the Devil. (Another reason was that in the colder climate of Britain, refrigeration wasn't needed as much. Perishable food was kept in a "safe" that hung on the wall outside the house.)

In Florida, where it is hot and humid, Dr. John Gorrie invented an ice machine to cool off his patients who suffered from high fevers. His machine air-conditioned the hospital *and* made ice. In 1851 Dr. Gorrie received the first U.S. refrigeration patent.

Early nonmechanical refrigerators dripped and smelled bad. They were wooden ice chests usually kept on the back porch. A piece of ice in the top shelf cooled the lower shelves. An iceman delivered ice to each house and often tracked in mud. People wanted something less messy that worked better.

General Electric offered the first household refrigerator with an automatic compressor in 1917. The compressors were large and noisy. Rich people bought refrigerators anyway. As mass production techniques improved, more companies entered the business and hired industrial designers to modernize refrigerators, make them quieter, and increase sales. General Electric had been offering a model called the Monitor Top. It had a compressor the size of a hatbox right on top of the unit (Fig. 2.6). The company hired Henry Dreyfuss to redesign its refrigerator in 1934. He took the compressor off the top, enclosed it in the base, got rid of the spindly legs, and created a handsome new unit—the Flat-Top.

Sears asked him to redesign its line of refrigerators, but Dreyfuss refused. Although he was designing washing machines for Sears, he felt it would be wrong to work on refrigerators while he was under contract to redesign that appliance for GE, so he recommended his friend and colleague Raymond Loewy.

Loewy had immigrated to the United States from France. With his background in art and engineering, he entered the new field of industrial design. Soon he was designing everything from cars, locomotives, and lipsticks to household appliances. The Coldspot refrigerator for Sears was one of his early successes and launched his career (Fig. 2.7).

Loewy applied the principle of streamlining and gave the refrigerator a tall, sleek shape. First he drew small sketches.

Then he constructed a full-size model. For the shelves he used a material he had been working with in designing cars—perforated aluminum. The Coldspot was attractive, rust-resistant, and inexpensive. Other companies imitated his idea. Details like the hardware were important to Loewy. "The new latch was . . . as well designed as if it had been intended to be the door handle of an expensive automobile," he wrote. "The name plate looked like a fine piece of jewelry." The overall effect was one of quality and simplicity. Customers loved it and sales tripled.

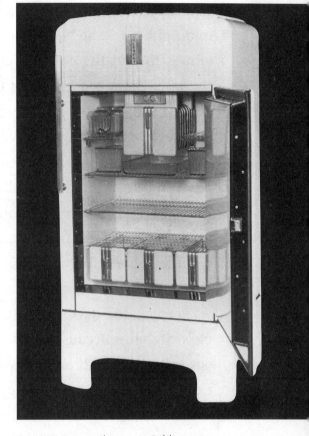

Fig. 2.7. Raymond Loewy's Coldspot refrigerator for Sears, 1935

In the following years, refrigerators got bigger and better. They grew from six cubic feet of storage space to sixteen, eighteen, twenty-two, and thirty feet. As companies competed to increase sales, they offered refrigerators with more features: horizontal units hung like cabinets, separate freezer compartments, shelves on the doors, self-defrosting models, automatic ice makers, glass shelves that pulled out on rollers.

In the 1950s Henry Dreyfuss imagined something even better.

One night as he was poking through his refrigerator for a midnight snack, he had to reach way back behind bottles and containers to find the cheddar cheese. *Why not revolving shelves?* he thought. He talked his client GE into making some experimental models and put one in his own kitchen.

Dreyfuss was delighted. Whenever he went to the refrigerator for a midnight snack, he could spin the shelves and find anything he wanted. But his housekeeper didn't like the spinning shelves because she couldn't easily find what she wanted on them. For years she had been keeping items in the same place on the same shelves. GE was equally unenthusiastic and scrapped the idea.

Refrigerator doors are often used as bulletin boards in people's kitchens. Because notes are fastened on them with magnets, designers have come up with other advances. The Sub-Zero Company now puts out a refrigerator with a built-in chalkboard panel so people can write their notes directly on the door! Some inventors want to go further and turn the doors into electronic message centers with flashing words, such as "I'm out jogging. Help yourself to a snack. I'll be home by 4:30. Love, Mom." Another new idea is to mount a television set in the freezer door to save space on countertops.

These days refrigerators are using less energy than guzzlers of the past. For example, it can cost the same to run a refrigerator for a year as to light a seventy-five-watt bulb. Energy-saving switches, introduced in 1978, turn on little heaters to get rid of condensation.

Bulky refrigerators have always posed a problem for designers who want to make kitchens appear seamless and streamlined. The solution? Having several small, compact refrigerators scattered throughout the kitchen. These modules fit under counters and look like kitchen cabinets. Each one serves a special purpose. The module containing vegetables can be placed next to the sink. A little refrigerator near the back door enables kids to help themselves to cold drinks and snacks without tracking through the house.

3

Cleaning Up

Laundry Machines

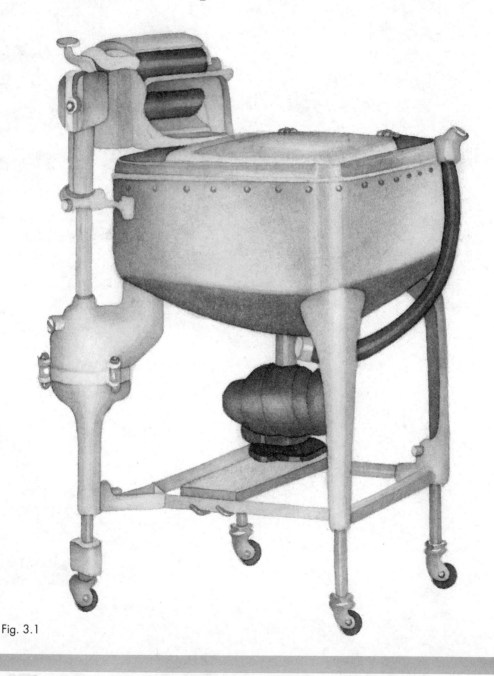

Fig. 3.1

Cleaning up the living space has traditionally been a woman's job. Throughout history women have been expected to wash clothes, beat carpets, and scrub floors in order to keep their homes and families clean and comfortable. Electrical appliances invented in the twentieth century make "women's work" easier and less time-consuming.

Before there were washing machines, women did the wash by hand. The first "washing machine" was a flat rock near a running stream. Women rubbed clothes against the rock to remove dirt. Millions of women still wash their family's clothes this way. It is hard work and can take several days. During the Middle Ages in England, laundering was done a couple of times a year as a group activity. In good weather washerwomen enjoyed doing their work together and having the chance to talk to their friends.

In rich households during the seventeenth century, servants did the laundry and washerwomen came into the home to assist them. In more modest homes the mistress and her maid did the laundry themselves. They wrung out the clothes by hand and hung them to dry on lines, or they spread them to dry over sweet-smelling bushes. Scottish women did the wash by stamping on it with bare feet in a bucket of water. While they worked, they danced up and down and sang rousing songs.

Because it was considered "women's work," laundering was thought to be shameful work for a man. If a man didn't have enough money to hire a washerwoman, he did his laundry secretly in the middle of the night so that the neighbors wouldn't find out. A drawing by the artist George Cruikshank in 1824 shows a poor widower washing his children's clothes by candle-light as they sleep.

Commercial laundries were founded in the 1830s in American seaports and gold-mining towns. These laundries were mainly for men who didn't have wives or mothers nearby to wash their shirts and collars. Most miners in California during the gold rush of 1848 washed their own shirts. Sunday was laundry day (Fig. 3.2). The miners set Sunday apart as a special day. Some of them observed the Christian Sabbath and attended services outdoors, or did chores such as shopping for weekly supplies. They spent Sunday having a good time, too—drinking in the saloons, gambling, and, if they had found gold, celebrating.

Rich gold miners who didn't have a laundry nearby sent their shirts out to be washed, starched, and ironed—in Hong Kong, China! It cost as much as a dollar a shirt and took two to four months for the shirts to make the round-trip.

Chinese men who had come to California to mine gold were

Fig. 3.2. Gold miners washing their shirts

treated terribly by prejudiced white miners, who only allowed them to mine in dirt that had already been worked over. The Chinese saw another opportunity for making money—and opened laundries. Although men didn't usually do laundry in China, in the United States it was acceptable.

Pioneer women on the prairie also had a hard time keeping their families in clean clothes. Monday was their wash day. Women needed most of the week to finish the laundry, and clothes had to be clean by Sunday for church. They, too, probably chose to wash on the same day so that they could keep one another company. Water had to be lugged in heavy buckets from a nearby well and boiled over a fire. The women scrubbed the clothes on washboards, wrung them out by hand, then hung them out to dry. The journals and diaries of pioneer housewives reveal that the task they hated most was laundry.

Many nineteenth-century inventors worked on the idea of a mechanically operated washing machine. The Cataract washer was created in 1831. An advertisement for it in a catalog showed a weary-looking woman turning the crank of a cylinder (Fig 3.3). "This Machine dispenses entirely with the washboard," boasted the ad. "The Machine is simple in construction and management—a child can use it . . . Send your Dirty Clothes and test it." (It is not known how many people answered the ad.)

By 1875 about two thousand patents for mechanical washers had been taken out in the United States. One of these was called the Pastime. It looked like a wooden washtub on legs. It was the first washing machine made by Maytag, a company that had been producing farm equipment. The ad showed a young boy turning the handle of the lid of the washer.

At the end of the nineteenth century, laundering was usually done in the kitchen. A New York writer described the scene in his house:

> *On laundry days not much cooking was done because the copper clothes boiler was steaming on the stove all day, with the laundress trotting back and forth from the tubs to the boiler, fishing the boiled laundry out of the bubbling water with a long "clothes stick" which had become soft and soggy from the constant hot water dips.*

By the turn of the century, many families had hired a laundress or regularly sent their wash out to commercial laundries. The first power-operated washers for home use were invented in 1910. Early models had a wringer on top to prepare the clothes for drying. The person doing the wash (usually the housewife or laundress) pushed the clothes between two rollers and at the same time turned the crank to squeeze out excess water.

Maytag's model was called the Hired Girl Washer, because in those days washing machines were considered substitutes for servants. From 1880 to 1920 more and more women were working in shops, offices, and factories, and there were fewer maids. Housewives had to do the chores themselves. They wanted machines to make the task easier.

The chore of doing laundry changed dramatically when Howard Snyder invented the electric washing machine in 1922.

Fig. 3.3. The Cataract washer, shown in *G. & D. Cook and Company's Illustrated Catalog of Carriages and Special Business Advertiser 1869*

Snyder worked for the Maytag Company. He was a mechanic who liked to fool with machinery and "fix things up." At that time Maytag was producing two kinds of hand-powered washers. One was a cylinder type. The other had wooden pegs inside that dragged the clothes through the water. Frederick Maytag, founder of the company, wanted a better washer. Snyder came to him one day and said, "I've got it."

He designed an agitator type of washer that is still in use. (Blades forcing water through the clothes get them cleaner.) The Maytag Gyrafoam washer was a great success. It was made of aluminum and known as the gray ghost because of its color (Fig. 3.1). Other companies copied Snyder's idea and made their own electric washers.

But customers complained that the washers looked like factory equipment. They wanted more attractive appliances in their homes. Once again manufacturers hired industrial designers to develop new options. Henry Dreyfuss worked for Sears. His first concern was to design a washer that would be easy to operate. Dreyfuss took one of Sears's old automatic models to his farm and washed clothes for two days before starting on the design. He realized that the controls were arranged inconveniently. They were positioned in different places on the machine, next to the parts they operated. The control for the wringer was on the top of the machine, next to the wringer, and the control for the spigot that released water from the washtub was at the bottom of the unit. Dreyfuss moved all the controls to the wringer arm on the top of the washer and called his machine the Toperator. Applying the principles of streamlining, Dreyfuss enclosed the tub and motor in a blue-green enamel shell. Three strips of metal hid dirt-catching bolts, and the inside of the tub stayed white. Dreyfuss said, "The place where the clothes were to be washed should look as clean as possible."

At last satisfied with his design, Dreyfuss took the working model to the executives' fancy wood-paneled office, complete with an Oriental rug, and nervously demonstrated the machine. First he pushed a control to start the agitator, then added soap to make suds. But by accident, instead of touching the next lever, which operated the wringer, he touched the one that emptied the tub. Soapsuds flooded the floor and the executives went running.

Another early industrial designer, Harold Van Doren, went to work for the Maytag Company. He redesigned Maytag's gray ghost washer and encased it in white enamel. After studying color and its effects on people, Van Doren chose white because it "suggests purity, cleanliness, sanitation." His new machine, called the Master, was easier to clean, safer to operate, and could hold a larger load of wash. It sold so well that Maytag became one of the leading producers of washing machines in the world.

Bendix entered the competition and came up with an automatic washer without a wringer. Instead, it had a drum inside that spun the excess water out of the clothes. A glass window in the door on the front panel allowed the user to watch the laundry tumbling around. It was still necessary to hang clothes on a line to dry them.

During World War II many companies stopped producing washing machines and manufactured goods for the defense effort. But after the war there was a greater demand than ever for home appliances.

The first automatic dryers were introduced by Sears in 1949 and Maytag in 1951. These new appliances provided a mechanical way of drying laundry. Before dryers were invented, clothes were hung outside on a line or were spread out on hedges. As the water evaporated, the clothes dried. Good weather made a difference. If the day was warm and breezy, the clothes dried faster. Dryers worked on the same principle but speeded up the process. Heated air tumbled through the damp laundry, causing the moisture to evaporate. The source of heat was either gas or electricity.

From the 1950s on, dryers became more complex and efficient. Various settings offered a range of temperatures appropriate for different kinds of fabrics. Sensors measured the amount of moisture in the clothes and a buzzer sounded when the laundry was done.

Dryers and washing machines were produced in sets. They came in the same sizes, shapes, and colors, and were designed to be placed side by side. Smaller washer and dryer "twins" could be stacked, one above the other.

More developments followed: Washers were top loading, cycles were developed for new fabrics, push buttons arranged on a panel replaced old-fashioned knobs, and laundry machines were offered in a choice of colors—pink, yellow, avocado green, gold, and copper.

Today customers for washers and dryers once again prefer white. They are also concerned about the environment and want machines that conserve natural resources. A Suds Saver washer reuses water. Dryers shut off automatically to save energy.

Yet for all the refinements that have been made in gas and electric dryers, people still enjoy the smell of sheets and clothes dried in the sun and fresh air.

Irons

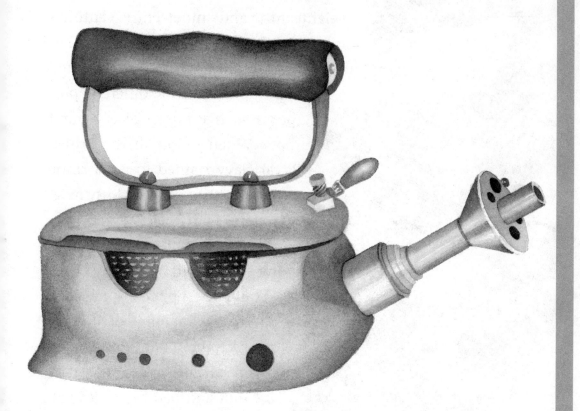

Fig. 3.4

The earliest tools for smoothing out wrinkled clothes were stones heated in the fire or in boiling water. The Vikings used mushroom-shaped glass objects called slickenstones to press away creases. A big pressing machine called the mangle was invented in the eighteenth century, then improved a hundred years later during the Industrial Revolution. In Britain during the nineteenth century, the work was sometimes done with wooden rollers.

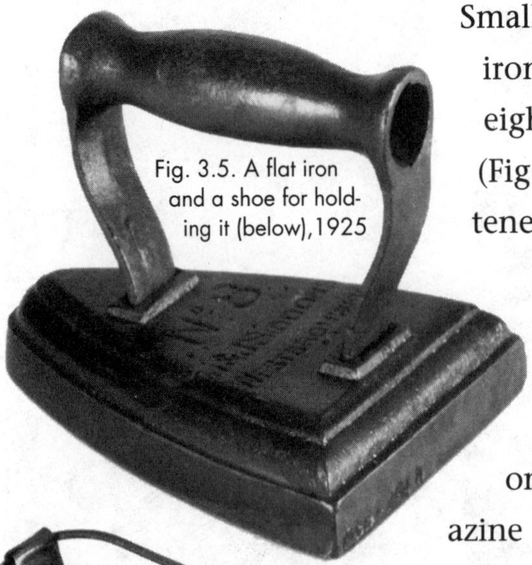

Fig. 3.5. A flat iron and a shoe for holding it (below), 1925

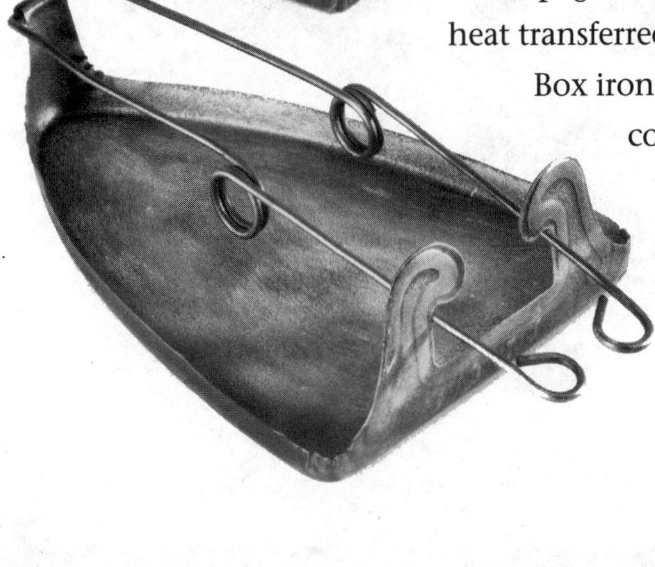

Small handheld irons (actually made of iron) were also manufactured in the eighteenth and nineteenth centuries (Fig 3.5). The weight of the hot iron flattened fabric. Irons came in assorted shapes and sizes for different purposes, such as pressing sleeves and hats. When sailors in the British Royal Navy wanted to get a shine on their pants, they pressed glossy magazine pages along with their trousers. The heat transferred the shine to the cloth.

Box irons were hollow (Fig. 3.6). They contained a piece of preheated iron or a lump of coal to keep them hot. Irons heated in the fireplace collected soot and had to be cleaned. An improvement came with

Fig. 3.6. Canon charcoal-heated flat iron with bellows, circa 1850

the sadiron, which could be heated on the stove. Sadirons were oval shaped. The bottom part was called the soleplate. Sadirons got their name not because ironing was a task that many women hated but because the word *sad* meant "solid." Sadirons were priced according to how much they weighed; the best ones were the heaviest ones. In 1871 Mrs. Mary Francis Potts improved on the sadiron by designing a detachable wooden handle. The Mrs. Potts' iron allowed many soleplates to be heated on the stove at one time (perhaps giving rise to the phrase "many irons in the fire") while the handle stayed cool.

Next came self-heating irons, which were fueled with natural gas, gasoline, or alcohol—and which often exploded. Although an electric iron was patented in 1882, it didn't become widely used until the beginning of the twentieth century, when electricity became available in homes.

Fig. 3.7. Steam-O-Matic iron, 1939; aluminum and plastic

Early electric irons looked like sadirons but instead of wooden handles had ones made from a resin material called Bakelite. Housewives loved these appliances because they made ironing faster and easier. As iron manufacturers competed for customers, they paid more attention to restyling their products and once again turned to industrial designers for help.

Harold Van Doren designed a streamlined iron for Westinghouse that started a trend. The Bakelite handle was curved to better fit a woman's hand. A dial regulated different temperature settings for various fabrics. Sunbeam produced a steam iron called the Steam-O-Matic. Steam, rather than the weight of the hot iron, pressed wrinkles from the clothes (Fig. 3.7). Irons became lighter and were made of aluminum rather than heavier materials. One company manufactured an iron made of solid glass. Thermostats provided temperature control and lights flashed on, signaling when the iron was hot. Cordless irons appeared as early as 1948 but proved to be a nuisance because they had to be returned to their base for reheating—just like the old-fashioned sadirons.

Ordinary household objects like irons and the ordinary women who used them inspired great artists. In 1767 Henry Robert Morland painted *A Servant Ironing,* showing a lovely young woman tenderly pressing a handkerchief with a box iron. Edgar Degas more realistically expressed the fatigue of ironing in his painting *Two Laundresses.* One of the women leans on the iron with all her might, while the other stretches and yawns and reaches for a bottle of wine.

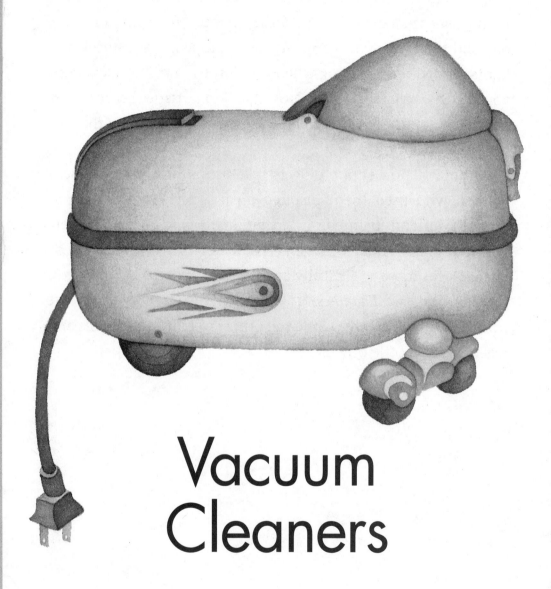

Vacuum
Cleaners

Fig. 3.8.

But has any fine artist ever painted a woman vacuuming? Maybe not, though a commercial artist at the turn of the century drew a manservant in a tuxedo vacuuming the drapes in a fancy house.

Before there were vacuum cleaners, people (mainly women) cleaned floors with mops, brushes, and brooms. Twig brooms date back to 2300 B.C. and are still used in parts of the world. In Scotland during the eighteenth century, women mopped with their bare feet. They spread a wet cloth on the floor, hitched up their skirts, and shuffled back and forth, moving the cloth around, then washing it out. Some people still mop with their feet.

Women were expected to take pride in a clean house and be professional homemakers. "Cleanliness is indeed next to godliness," preached John Wesley in the nineteenth century. People were also learning that dirt can spread disease. But cleaning up was a never-ending job. How could it be done more quickly and easily?

In the United States the carpet sweeper was invented in 1858 by H. H. Herrick. Cleaning was done by a rotating brush, turned by a crank. A sweeper that was to become popular was manufactured by Melville R. Bissell in 1876 (Fig. 3.9). But inventors kept working on the idea of a vacuum cleaner. Some were hand operated; another kind had an electric motor that blew dust through a pipe into a box.

A London engineer, Cecil Booth, saw a demonstration of one of these early machines and believed he could improve on it by using suction. Back in his office he experimented. His partner, Charles Hitchins, watched as Booth "spread a white handkerchief

Fig. 3.9. Bissell's carpet sweeper. Bissell began making carpet sweepers in 1876.

on the top of the carpet, went down on his knees, and sucked on the top of the handkerchief for a few seconds, then took the handkerchief up. On the side which had lain on the carpet there was a dirty mark, which was dust." Booth performed a similar experiment in a London restaurant. He began sucking the back of his plush chair, shocking the other diners but proving (despite a fit of coughing and choking) that dirt could be removed by suction.

Booth and Hutchins began to manufacture cleaning devices known as Booth's Original Vacuum Cleaner Pumps or Puffing Billies. The big pumps were mounted on horse-drawn carts and taken to hotels, stores, and the households of the rich. Uniformed operators carried the hoses inside and cleaned. Hostesses gave tea parties on the days the crews arrived so that their friends could watch. Booth was even asked to vacuum the carpet at Westminster Abbey for the coronation of Edward VII. Afterward the king and queen became his customers and installed a centrally powered cleaning system at Buckingham Palace.

In the United States the first "portable" electric vacuum was invented in 1906. It weighed ninety-two pounds. Then a janitor named James Murray Spangler came up with something better. Spangler worked in a department store in Canton, Ohio, and used a broom and carpet sweeper at his job. Because dust made him cough, he combined the new idea of removing dirt by suction with the mechanics of a carpet sweeper. His first vacuum cleaner was a crude thing made of tin and wood, with a pillowcase for the dust bag—but it worked!

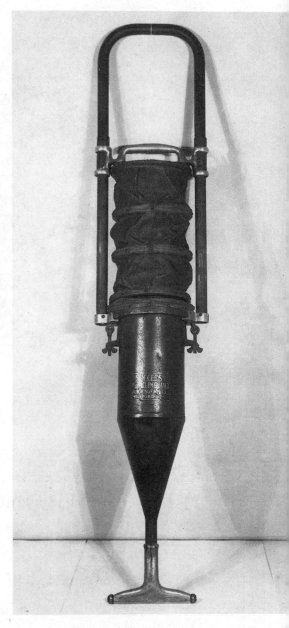

Fig. 3.10. Success hand vacuum cleaner made by the Hutchinson Manufacturing Company in Pennsylvania, 1910. Pumping the handle operated the bellows, which created the suction.

Fig. 3.11. Kotten suction sweeper, 1910. Standing on the platform and rocking from side to side, like on a teeter-totter, made the sweeper work.

Spangler didn't have the money or know-how to manufacture his invention. He showed it to a boyhood friend, William H. Hoover, who had a tannery business nearby. Hoover bought the patent and a new company was formed, with Spangler in charge of production. The Model O Hoover came out in 1908. It was made of tin, weighed only forty pounds, and had cleaning tool attachments. A dull gray bag with a cheesecloth liner held the dirt. The Hoover depended on electricity, but not everyone had electricity in 1908. So manual vacuum sweepers (Fig. 3.10) and the Kotten suction sweeper (Fig. 3.11) were still being used.

A new model came out in 1926. This one used beater bars to loosen the dirt in the carpet. The Hoover slogan was: "It beats, as it sweeps, as it cleans." More improvements followed, including disposable paper dust bags and headlights. The appliances were so popular that the company opened a branch in Britain. There, as in many places in the world, vacuuming is still called Hoovering.

Mr. Hoover knew how to market vacuums. In the United States he sent teams of salesmen door-to-door to demonstrate the new machines to housewives. The salesmen sang "The Hoover Song": *All the dirt, all the grit / Hoover gets it, every bit.*

Other companies, including Eureka and Electrolux, began manufacturing vacuums and copied Hoover's sales technique. An ad in the *Ladies' Home Journal* in 1928 showed a smiling salesman, with his hat in hand, standing at a housewife's doorstep. The message said, "Welcome the Eureka Man—he brings new standards of home sanitation."

In the mid-1930s, during the Great Depression, people didn't have jobs or money to buy things. Companies that produced vacuum cleaners feared going out of business. How could they increase their sales? They had to offer a more attractive, lower-priced product that housewives would find irresistible. The Hoover Company hired Henry Dreyfuss to redesign its original model, which by now looked no different from the other vacuums on the market.

Dreyfuss did more than give the Hoover a face-lift. Working with engineers, he completely rethought the appliance so that it would work more efficiently. First he made the vacuum lighter by constructing it from magnesium and Bakelite instead of aluminum. Other innovations included a clip-on cord plug, a signal to empty the bag when it was full, and an adjustable handgrip.

Dreyfuss used the principle of streamlining and gave the new Model 150 a lower, sleeker look (Fig. 3.12). He enclosed the motor in a teardrop shape resembling the cab of a high-speed train. The

Fig. 3.12. Hoover Model 150, designed by Henry Dreyfuss, 1936

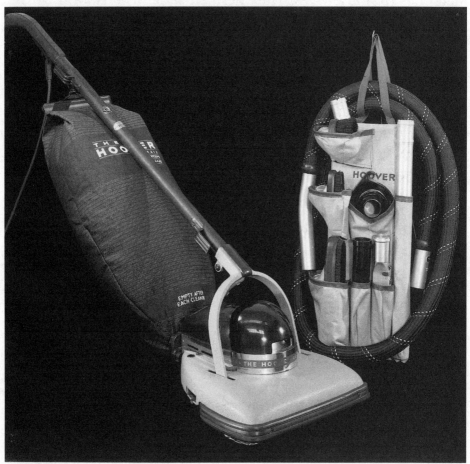

edges of the vacuum were rounded so that they wouldn't scratch furniture. Dreyfuss changed the color of the dust bag from black and silver to "stratosphere grey and blue"—the colors he had used for the interior of a locomotive he designed. The Model 150 was a landmark in vacuum design and went unchanged for many years.

During World War II the Hoover Company, like many other manufacturers, turned to producing military goods. After the war Hoover went back to making vacuum cleaners and came up with a canister cleaner that quietly rolled along the carpet, a stretch-type cord, and lighter vacuums that worked at higher speeds.

The Eureka Company introduced the Mighty Mite vacuum cleaner in 1982. It was designed by Samuel E. Hohulin and Kenneth R. Parker. Weighing in at eight pounds, fourteen ounces, it was light enough to be carried around with one hand or on a shoulder strap. Its bright colors—red, blue, and green—and large wheels made it look like a toy. But ads said, "This is no toy. The new Eureka Mighty Mite is a mighty serious vacuum cleaner."

With a tool like the Mighty Mite, was cleaning up becoming fun? Fun or not, it certainly was becoming a responsibility for *both* sexes. Traditions changed in the second part of the twentieth century as more and more women entered the workforce. Today everyone shares household duties.

4

"Hello! Are You There?"

Telephones

Fig. 4.1.

We need to communicate. We want to express our feelings, exchange information, make plans and appointments, or order things. Sometimes in an emergency we have to call for help. What did we do before there were telephones?

In earliest times people sent smoke signals or beat drums to communicate over long distances. Before there were written words, they painted pictures to describe events. The alphabets of many languages developed from pictorial marks or characters. It is not known for sure who invented letter writing, but letters are mentioned in the Bible (in the New Testament they are called epistles). The ancient Egyptians wrote letters on rolls of papyrus (a kind of paper) and linen. The Greeks had a special class of people who wrote letters, but those letters were more like speeches than conversation. The Romans, who had a vast empire, used letter writing as a way to send information about business and war to one another. Messengers delivered the mail on foot then—and later, in chariots. During the Middle Ages most letters were written in Latin by scholars, since few people could read or write.

Letter writing became more widespread and personal during the seventeenth century and reached a peak in the eighteenth century in western Europe. It was the "'letterwritingest' of ages," according to one historian. Everybody wrote letters, sometimes more than once a day! For instance, two French people who lived in the same house and saw each other daily nevertheless exchanged long letters before breakfast.

But sending mail for any distance was expensive and slow. It traveled in ships and horse-drawn stagecoaches. In America during Colonial times, a "postwalker" carried letters in a pouch on his back. At the beginning of the nineteenth century, the U.S. mail was transported by a rider on horseback, then in stage wagons and, starting in 1832, on trains. When the West began to open up, the Pony Express promised to speed up mail delivery between Missouri and California. But the Pony Express only lasted for nineteen months. The riders were strong young men who rode in relays. Yet it took ten days for a letter to reach Sacramento, California, from Saint Joseph, Missouri. How could people communicate faster?

The telegraph was invented in 1844 by Samuel F. B. Morse. Operators tapped out coded messages that were transmitted over a wire. Only the operators were able to translate the code, and just one message could be sent at a time. Thomas A. Edison, an inventor, and Alexander Graham Bell, a teacher of the deaf, worked on improving the telegraph.

Bell had also been experimenting with an idea for an instrument that could transmit spoken words rather than code. He began working on that device at his parents' home in Brantford, Ontario, and continued in Boston, Massachusetts. Bell collaborated with Thomas A. Watson, an artisan who was good at constructing electrical gadgets. One night, in their Boston workshop, Bell transmitted sound over a wire. The next day Watson built the first telephone. Bell filed a patent for it on February 14, 1876. Three days later he made his first phone call to Watson.

Meanwhile, in Highland Park, Illinois, Elisha Gray was also working on a telephone device. He filed his patent the very same day Bell did—a few hours later. Western Union bought Gray's patent and challenged Bell in court but eventually lost.

Bell demonstrated his phone at the Centennial Exhibition in Philadelphia in 1876. People marveled at it. Bell and Watson kept working on it, and gave demonstrations and lectures. One evening in Massachusetts, Bell was in Salem and Watson was in Boston. From the phone box came Watson's voice shouting, "Hoy! Hoy!" —the telephonic greeting Bell insisted upon all his life (Fig. 4.2). The next year Bell and his partners founded the Bell Telephone Company. They decided that the phones would be leased, not sold, to the customers. People were soon clamoring for phones, though some were afraid of the speaking instrument. They thought that hearing voices without seeing anyone was a sign of insanity or that it proved the presence of otherworldly spirits.

A Boston banker bought the first pair of telephones, called

Fig. 4.2. Liquid telephone, 1876. On March 10, 1876, Alexander Graham Bell spoke the first words over this telephone, his invention: "Mr. Watson, come here. I want you."

Fig. 4.3. Commercial Set, 1877.
The opening served as both receiver and transmitter.

the Commercial Set, in 1877. (It took two to make a conversation.) These were shaped like boxes, with an opening for both listening and speaking (Fig. 4.3). The banker had a private line strung between his office and his house so that he could let his wife know when he was coming home to dinner.

Within a year thirteen hundred phones were in use. The first central switchboard was established in New Haven, Connecticut. Boys who had worked in telegraph offices were the first telephone operators. They dragged wires across the floor, connecting callers with one another. The boys mischievously crossed wires, mixing up calls, and even insulted the callers. Soon they were replaced by "more responsible" young women.

Watson continued to improve the design and mechanics of the phone. The next model was called the Butterstamp (Fig. 4.4). It was mounted to the wall and had a combined ear-and-mouthpiece receiver that looked like the butterstamp found in farmers' kitchens. One person could talk while the other listened. The Wall Set, introduced in 1878, had a second receiver, allowing two people to talk and listen at the same time. But clicks and buzzes made it hard to hear. People shouted at each other. Customers made a call by winding the phone with a crank that rang a bell. Then they said, "Are you there?" Thomas Edison, who was working on improving the quality of the sound, shortened the greeting. One day in his lab while he was making tests, he picked up the phone and simply shouted, "Hello!" And it became the new way to begin a conversation or answer the phone all over the United States. In other parts of the world, people have different telephone greetings. The French say, *"Âllo!"* The Germans say, *"Hallo"* or *"Bitte?"* (which means "Please?"). In Italy the

Fig. 4.4. Butterstamp phone, 1878. The first set with a hand-held receiver/transmitter was in service when the first switchboard opened in New Haven, Connecticut.

familiar greeting is *"Pronto!"* as in "Ready!" (to listen). The Spanish and Argentineans say, *"¡Diga!"* (for "Speak up!"). And in Mexico, *"¡Bueno!"* (meaning "Good!" [I'm ready to listen to you]) is the way people answer the phone.

Wall-mounted phones were the type used in homes until the turn of the century. The ringing part was in a box of its own. Cowbells or sleigh bells announced a call. (Bell himself hated the continuous jangle and refused to have a phone in his study.)

Businesspeople wanted phones on their desks. The Candlestick phone appeared in the 1890s and was used through the 1920s (Fig. 4.1). There were problems with it, though. It was made of brass and was heavy. Often it tipped over. The receiver sometimes fell off the hook. The Desk Set, also known as the French Phone, was a better model (Fig. 4.5). It had originated in France, where U.S. soldiers saw it in use during World War I. Squat and black, it had a single handheld piece for listening and speaking.

So many people were using phones that operators were kept constantly busy plugging and unplugging lines. Almon Strowger, a grumpy undertaker in Kansas City, believed operators were purposely sending his calls to a competitor. He was determined to devise a "girlless, cussless telephone" and invented the first automatic dialing system. Although Strowger and others were eventually able to dial their own numbers, operators remained on the job.

Dials were put on the French Phones and Candlestick phones, but there were other problems. The ringing part was still in a box on the wall, and the instruments looked out of place in living

Fig. 4.5. Desk Set telephone, 1928

rooms. Some people kept their phones in cabinets or plaster globes of the world or concealed within a doll's fluffy skirt, which covered a phone like a tea cozy.

In 1930 Bell Telephone Laboratories invited ten artists and craftsmen to submit sketches of what the modern phone should look like. Henry Dreyfuss was one of the ten. He had just opened his office (with only a borrowed card table and folding chairs) and was flattered to be included in the competition. But he believed that a phone had to be designed from the inside out, and he wanted to work with technicians at Bell. His request was refused. After a few months no one had won the contest—and so Dreyfuss was given a chance. (All of the other designs turned out to be impractical.)

Dreyfuss began his research by going on rounds with a repairman to see how people used their phones and where they put them. After making hundreds of drawings and many models, he came up with the Series 300, which went into production in 1937. It was a black compact phone made in metal, then later in plastic. The bell was enclosed in the square base. The dial was clearly marked with letters and numbers.

Dreyfuss was inspired by a desk phone designed in 1930 by Jean Heiberg, a painter and sculptor, for the L. M. Ericsson Company in Sweden. The Ericsson phone was used throughout western Europe. The Model 300 (properly called the 302) became a standard item throughout the United States and went unchanged for nearly twenty years (Fig. 4.6).

In 1946 Bell again asked Dreyfuss to improve the phone design. The old handset, for instance, couldn't be comfortably cradled between a person's ear and shoulder. Dreyfuss studied measurements of two thousand human heads to determine the average space between a person's mouth and ear. "A good design," he said, "must start with an understanding of the man, woman or child who will eventually use the object . . . we must fit the machine to the man—not squeeze the man into the machine." Dreyfuss rejected many design concepts until he arrived at the Model 500. This new phone had

Fig. 4.6. Model 302 telephone, 1937

numbers outside the finger wheel so they wouldn't flicker as a person dialed. The characters were larger and easier to read. The volume of the ring could be adjusted.

In the 1950s Dreyfuss and his staff kept making improvements: Phones became available in colors as well as in black; push buttons replaced the circular dial so that calls could be made faster; the Princess phone, introduced mainly for women and girls, glowed in the dark. The Trimline appeared in 1965 and incorporated the dial, and later push buttons, in the handset. The phone was so graceful and sculptural that it was accepted in the collections of the Philadelphia Museum of Art and the Museum of Modern Art (Fig. 4.7). Dreyfuss realized that the telephone was capable of raising the public's level of good taste. "No other product reaches so many people so often," he said.

The Ericsson Company in Sweden introduced the world's first one-piece telephone, with a dial in the base. Produced in gorgeous colors like mint green and lemon yellow, it was strikingly beautiful and became a collector's item. Don Adams, starring as a bumbling spy in *Get Smart,* a popular television show from 1965 to 1970, used a similar one-piece phone hidden in the bottom of his shoe.

Lady Bird Johnson, wife of President Lyndon Johnson, wanted more beautiful pay phones for the national parks. She asked Dreyfuss and his firm to design them. The new phone booths were made mostly of glass. Shortly after they were installed, the rangers reported that many had been smashed to bits. Bull moose, viewing their reflections in the phone booths, thought

Fig. 4.7. Trimline telephone, 1968

they were seeing other bull moose and charged. The glass booths were replaced with concrete-encased structures.

Once it became technically feasible to unite the interior components of telephones, the exterior could take any form. Phones came in wacky new shapes—high heels, lips, Coke bottles, and Mickey Mouse. People now bought phones instead of renting them.

Dreyfuss invented the Picturephone in the 1960s. People placing a call could take pictures of themselves or anything else in their room and transmit the image. Maps and charts could be sent this way, too. Although the Picturephone was widely field-tested and scheduled for release in the early 1970s, the program was finally scrapped. The design was fine, but picture quality wasn't good enough because of technological limitations—and the Picturephone cost too much.

Although it never caught on, the Picturephone led the way for the fax. The facsimile machine was developed simultaneously in America and Japan. It was hooked up to the phone line and allowed callers to send an exact copy of a document or drawing. When the first international patent was taken out in 1968, it took six minutes to transmit each page. Today multiple pages can be faxed in a matter of minutes.

Phones went cordless in the 1980s. Cellular phones, which were portable, came on the market in 1983. Cell phones were first used by the military in the late 1960s for the Vietnam War. The military considered the cell phones as classified and the government didn't give permission for them to be released and developed for the general public until 1980. Calls could be made from anyplace—streets, cars, airplanes—to anywhere in the world that had compatible systems. The newest ones are only four inches long, small enough to slip into a pocket. The 900 cordless phone named Tell-Go runs off a home phone and can be used as far away from its home base as five to ten miles.

Another innovation is Caller ID. On the first ring the phone number of the person calling appears on a little screen above the dial. Eventually the person's name will come into view also. Then the person receiving the call can decide whether or not to pick up the receiver and say, "Hello!"

5

QWERTY?

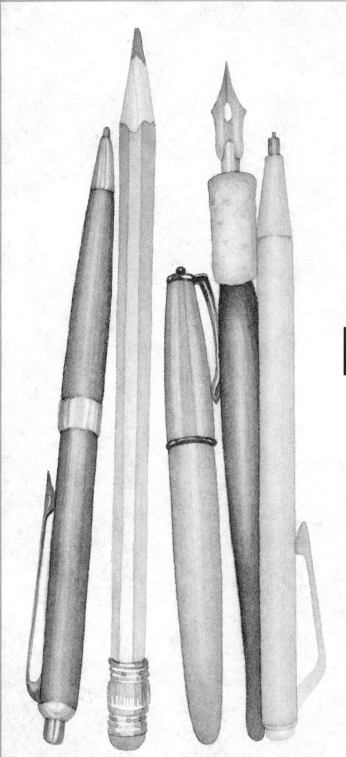

Pens
and
Pencils

Fig. 5.1

The ordinary desk or workstation may have as many as one hundred different objects on it, from simple things like pencils, pens, and paper clips to complex machines like typewriters and computers. These objects were all designed by someone and mass-produced. Who made these things? And why do they look the way they do?

The first pens were made from hollow reeds sharpened to a point and used to write on clay or wax tablets and animal skins. In the seventh century, quills from birds' feathers replaced reeds.

Steel nibs (pen points) were manufactured in the nineteenth century and were attached to holders. People kept using quills, however, until the 1860s. American schoolchildren were expected to make their own pens by sharpening goose quills with a penknife.

Meanwhile, inventors tried to add ink reservoirs to quills, but their experiments failed. Early fountain pens leaked and were unreliable. Sometimes they had too much ink, other times none at all. Lewis Edson Waterman, an insurance broker, invented a better fountain pen in 1884. The story goes that he lost a deal to a rival broker when his pen leaked all over a document he was about to sign. Waterman decided to make one that would work. He sold so many the first year that he abandoned the insurance business to make pens. His product was known for its quality. The British prime minister David Lloyd George signed the Treaty of Versailles in 1919 (at the end of World War I) with a solid gold Waterman pen. Waterman had a tradition of making pens that were artistic yet functional. The Ink-Vue in 1936 (Fig. 5.2) held more ink than other pens on the market and allowed the user to see the level in the decorative barrel.

George Safford Parker, a teacher in Wisconsin, also set out to make a better pen. He had been selling fountain pens to his students as a side job. When the pens didn't write properly (and they usually didn't), Parker repaired them. He spent so much time fixing pens that he finally created one of his own design and took out his first patent in 1888. A couple of years later he founded the Parker Pen Company.

His first successful pen was called the Lucky Curve. It was a "self-filling" pen and had a unique device that prevented it from leaking. Parker made other innovations: the first slip-on cap, a gold ring mounted on the top of a ladies' pen for attaching a ribbon, and a black rubber Snake Pen with a gold or silver green-eyed snake wound around the barrel and cap. (Some of these are considered valuable antiques today.) During World War I he invented the Trench Pen for American soldiers stationed abroad who wanted to write home. This pen featured black pigment pellets that converted water to ink.

In 1921 Parker introduced the Duofold, also known as Big Red because of its unusual orange-red color. (In those days most pens were black.) The Duofold was an instant hit. Sir Arthur Conan Doyle used his to write the adventures of Sherlock Holmes. The first Duofolds were made of red rubber then, later, plastic. They were guaranteed to last forever. To prove that the pens were unbreakable, they were dropped from planes, skyscrapers, and over

Fig. 5.2. A Waterman Ink-Vue pen and pencil set

the edge of the Grand Canyon. (How they were found again to prove their durability is not completely clear.)

Throughout the 1920s the pen business grew, then it slowed down during the Great Depression. To increase sales, the Wahl-Eversharp Company hired Henry Dreyfuss to design a new fountain pen. His creation, the Skyline, appeared in 1941. Tapered at the end, its form suggested the new skyscrapers going up in New York at the time.

A year earlier Kenneth Parker had worked with industrial designers to create the Parker 51, a fountain pen with fast-drying ink. "Writes dry with wet ink!" read the advertisement in magazines. "Like a pen from another planet." The Parker 51 had a sleek rocketlike shape. It looked modern, was comfortable to hold, and was considered a classic of streamlined design (Fig. 5.3).

The ballpoint pen was introduced to Americans in the mid-1940s. The first one had been invented in 1888. A better model was patented in 1938 by Laszlo Biro, a Hungarian artist and inventor living in Argentina. Biro collaborated with his brother, a chemist. They figured out how to feed a fast-drying ink to a steel ball, which replaced the nib. After World War II the pen

Fig. 5.3. A Parker 51 fountain pen

was mass-produced by Milton Reynolds in Chicago. Rumors spread that the newfangled pen could write underwater. Customers lined up around a department store in New York to buy them, and twenty-five thousand were sold in one week. But ink from the pens leaked in pockets and smeared on paper. Dissatisfied customers returned their pens and demanded their money back.

Eventually ballpoint pens were improved. Parker brought out the Jotter in 1954. It had a textured ball that gripped the surface of the paper, an ink cartridge, and refills with different-sized points. It was a great success and still sells well.

A Frenchman, Marcel Bich, made a model with a clear plastic casing. He sold his Bic Crystal as the first disposable pen in 1958.

Today many companies make inexpensive ballpoint pens.

The ones designed for astronauts can write at any angle, even upside down, without leaking or smearing. Other updates include the fiber-tip pen (first produced by Pentel in Japan), highlighters, and ballpoint pens that write in more than one color. One of the newest items on the market, DataPen, features a side panel with an electronic organizer, clock, calculator, and one-hundred-year calendar. "DataPen can do almost everything but talk," wrote a reviewer in the *Los Angeles Times*.

Although we generally learn to use pencils before we use pens, the pencil was a later invention. Perhaps the most common instrument for writing and drawing is the pencil.

In earliest times people used burnt coal or sticks to draw pictures on the walls of caves. The Greeks and Romans had pencil brushes called *penicillum*. They resembled tiny watercolor brushes. These pointed instruments had shaped tufts of animal hairs inserted into hollow reeds, the way lead is inserted into a mechanical pencil. First the Romans ruled lines on their papyrus scrolls with a lead-filled stylus, another type of pointed instrument. Then they wrote words across the lines with their *penicillum* dipped in crude inks. Afterward they erased the lines. The Egyptians had pencil brushes, too, that were about the size of today's seven-inch pencils.

The first known use of a lead pencil was in 1565, when Konrad Gesner wrote a book in which he described and illustrated a new kind of writing instrument. It had "a sort of lead . . . shaved to a point and inserted in a wooden handle."

A year earlier pure graphite had been discovered in the

Cumberland hills in England. The substance was called *plumbago,* meaning "that which acts (writes) like lead." Sticks of it were sold in London as "marking stones." By the end of the sixteenth century, graphite *(plumbago)* was well known throughout Europe. The problem was how to hold it for writing without soiling fingers. Sometimes graphite was wrapped in sheepskin, or a piece was pushed into a hollow twig or straw and bound with string. In the seventeenth century, rods of graphite were enclosed in sticks of pine and cedar and glued so they wouldn't fall out.

In 1795 when war prevented France from importing graphite pencils from England, Napoléon ordered Nicolas-Jacques Conté, an engineer, to find another way to make pencils. Conté came up with a formula combining graphite dust, clay, and water. Depending on the amounts used, the pencil "leads" varied in hardness and made lines ranging from light to dark black. Actually, there was no lead at all in the "lead pencil"—and there still isn't today.

In America during the early 1800s, the first pencil-making establishment was founded by a schoolgirl in Massachusetts who liked to sketch and paint, and who had a few pieces of graphite. She crushed them into a powder, mixed it with glue, and stuffed it into a twig that she had hollowed out with a knitting needle. Later a man named Joseph W. Wade helped her manufacture pencils.

Henry David Thoreau, the poet, philosopher, and civil engineer, was also a pencil maker. His father and uncle started the business in the 1820s. Thoreau wanted to find out why American pencils weren't as good as the ones imported from England, Germany, and France. After much research he realized that grinding finer graphite dust produced higher-quality pencils. He invented a machine to do the job. As a result his family's company became known for manufacturing the best pencils in America.

At about the same time, Joseph Dixon established his pencil company in Salem, Massachusetts. At age thirteen Dixon watched the sailors on his father's ships dump graphite that had been used for ballast, or extra weight, into Massachusetts Bay. Dixon thought of putting the disposed graphite into pencils. When he grew up, he invented a machine for shaping pencils and opened a factory in Jersey City, New Jersey. With the Civil War the demand for pencils increased. Soldiers wanted to write letters home, but it was difficult for them to use quill pens and ink on the battlefield. Ink spilled when they carried it around. So they wrote to Dixon and asked to buy his "writing sticks." (Abraham Lincoln is said to have written his Gettysburg Address with a German pencil, but his tax on foreign goods helped the American pencil industry grow.) In 1873 Dixon bought the American Graphite Company of Ticonderoga, New York. That location became part of the company's name: the Joseph Dixon Ticonderoga Company.

Why are most pencils yellow? The tradition began in the late nineteenth century, when pencils were varnished to bring out the color of the wood. But if the wood was a poor quality, it was painted yellow, black, or blue. Yellow became associated with the Far East, where there were still supplies of good graphite. Also, yellow was considered a royal color in eastern Asia. Therefore, many customers believed a yellow pencil was best.

Manufacturers continued to try to improve the pencil. Horace

Hosmer, who finished pencils for the Eagle Pencil Company and Eberhard Faber, added an eraser to the end. (Not only did he put on rubber heads or erasers, he also polished, painted, or varnished the pencils, tied them in bundles of a dozen, and labeled the bundles. Only the inexpensive "penny pencils" had erasers.) The Joseph Dixon Ticonderoga Company also made school pencils with erasers, but some teachers disapproved. They thought erasers made it too easy for children to correct mistakes; therefore, they believed students would be less concerned about making errors. Another objection was that pupils, "especially boys," put the rubber tips into their mouths and then swapped pencils, increasing the chance of spreading disease.

By the 1880s molding machines made pencils in round and hexagonal shapes. The earliest pencils had been round, like brushes. Then, as the demand for pencils grew, woodworkers found it faster and easier to make square cases for the graphite. But people found it uncomfortable to hold square pencils. With the development of machines for making pencils a new question arose: What shape would make the most efficient use of machinery and materials? The hexagon, with six sides, seemed a sensible compromise. It wouldn't roll off a desk and it used less wood than a round pencil, according to the Joseph Dixon Ticonderoga Company. Companies now manufacture many different kinds of pencils for various purposes—drawing, drafting, and writing, among others.

The author John Steinbeck wrote in his journal: "For years I have looked for the perfect pencil. I have found very good ones but never the perfect one." Then he admitted, "And all the time it was not the pencils but me. A pencil that is all right some days is no good another day."

The only imperfection in the pencil was that it needed to be sharpened each time the point got dull. The mechanical pencil minimized that drawback. The first one was produced in 1822 by Sampson Mordan, an English engineer who also made pens. He called his invention an "ever-pointed" pencil. The lead was in a tube and as the point wore down, more lead pushed forward. In America James Bogardus, a watchmaker, patented a "forever pointed" pencil in 1833. Some models came with companion toothpicks and earspoons (used for cleaning the ears). But they were considered novelties rather than reliable writing instruments.

In the early 1900s Eversharp manufactured a mechanical pencil that wrote and felt like a real wood-cased pencil. By the 1920s it was selling so well that a hundred other companies jumped into the competition. Scripto marketed a mechanical pencil that cost ten cents. A selling point in those days was that sharpening pencils wasted valuable work time in the office.

Later, as the public became increasingly concerned about dwindling natural resources, pencil companies looked for substitutes for wood. In the 1980s Scripto developed a yellow plastic throwaway pencil. Today Berol USA makes Eagle Jeans pencils from recycled denim and Eagle Greenbacks from old money shredded by the Federal Reserve. Eberhard Faber's ECOwriter pencils are made from recycled cardboard and newspaper.

Typewriters

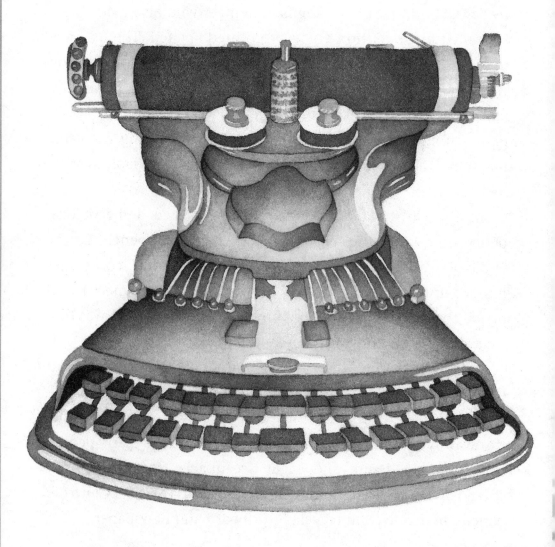

Fig. 5.4

In the nineteenth century, office clerks, who were mostly men, took hours to produce hand-written documents. Christopher Lathan Sholes, a printer and part-time inventor, and his associate Carlos Glidden wanted to speed up this process. They patented the first successful typewriter in 1868 and a few years later sold their patent to E. Remington & Sons.

Remington's factory manufactured guns and sewing machines but started mass-producing typewriters in 1874. The earliest model resembled a sewing machine. It had a foot-treadle carriage return and a black case decorated with pretty stenciled flowers to appeal to women, who were beginning to replace male clerks in the office. The New York YWCA began to offer typing lessons to women in 1881. The first class had only eight students, but in five years there were thousands of women "typewriters" (the word *typists* was coined afterward).

The first Sholes and Glidden Type Writer (manufactured by Remington) printed only capital letters and the person using the machine couldn't see what had been typed. The user had to lift up a hinged carriage to see the tiny letters, so these machines were known as blind writers. Sholes originally arranged the keyboard in alphabetical order. Once people learned the keyboard, they typed quickly and the keys often jammed. He fixed that by figuring out which pairs of letters occurred most frequently (such as *th, ed,* and *es*) and scattering them so that they wouldn't be next to each other. Typists were forced to slow down. The result was the QWERTY keyboard (named for the first six letters in the top row), still used today. (Remington salesmen liked the QWERTY keyboard because when the company demonstrated the new machine to skeptical customers, they could quickly find the letters of the word *typewriter* all in the same row.)

August Dvorak, a professor of education at the University of Washington, developed a different keyboard in 1936. He placed the most common letters on the "home row," the middle row of keys. In that continuous row he arranged the letters so that the left hand would type the vowels (*a, o, e, u, i*) and the right hand would type the most frequently used consonants (*d, h, t, n, s*). Dvorak thought his system would be easier on the fingers and make typing faster. But typists complained that it was too much trouble to learn a new keyboard and stuck with the QWERTY.

In 1878 the Remington No. 2 was introduced. This machine had the first shift key for writing lowercase as well as uppercase letters. It was so successful that many others jumped into the business of manufacturing typewriters.

One of these was a typewriter-ribbon maker named John Thomas Underwood. When he went to Remington to renew his contract, he was told that Remington had decided to make its own ribbons. Underwood was angry, so he decided to make his own typewriters. He invented the Underwood No. 1, which enabled users to see the words they were typing (Fig. 5.5). The visible format was a sensation, and soon other manufacturers produced similar models.

Mark Twain bought one of the first Remingtons. He called it a "curiosity-breeding little joker," and praised it because it "piles an awful stack of words on one page. It don't muss things or scatter

Fig. 5.5.
Underwood No. 1

ink blots around." Although Twain wrote longhand, his typist transcribed *Life on the Mississippi*, making it the first typewritten book manuscript to be submitted to a publisher. Twain also started the practice of double-spacing manuscripts to provide room for editors to write comments like "Awkward" and "Don't get this."

Lucy Maud Montgomery in Canada used her Empire manual typewriter to write *Anne of Green Gables* in 1905. In her journal she noted, "I typewrote it out on my old second-hand typewriter that never makes the capitals plain and won't print 'w' at all."

About that same time, Camillo Olivetti founded the first typewriter company in Italy. Olivetti had visited American factories to learn about production techniques. His main goal was good design. "A typewriter should not be a gewgaw for the drawing room, ornate or in questionable taste," he said. "It should have an appearance that is serious and elegant at the same time."

In the United States typewriters had exposed working parts and were large and black. For fifty years the basic shape hardly changed. Then, gradually, the parts were enclosed in a shell and the machines became lower and more streamlined. Industrial designers were hired to make typewriters more efficient and attractive. When the Royal Typewriter Company asked Henry Dreyfuss to think of ways to make the typewriter more appealing, he began his research by learning how to type. The glare from the polished metal bothered his eyes. (He had heard many typists complain of headaches.) So he made a machine with a dull finish to reduce eyestrain.

Dreyfuss also created a portable typewriter for Royal. "The most modern typewriter ever designed," proclaimed the ads. Portable typewriters weren't new, however. They had been available since the turn of the century. The Blickensderfer Company in Connecticut started marketing a portable in 1893. In its catalog it showed a journalist in a pith helmet riding a camel while typing on a portable Blick strapped to the camel's hump.

Although many companies made portable typewriters, Olivetti came up with the most beautiful and lightweight models, from the Lettera 22 to the Valentine, made of bright red molded plastic (Fig. 5.6).

IBM was jealous of Olivetti's reputation for good design and in the late 1940s hired Eliot Noyes, a designer who had studied at Harvard with Marcel Breuer and Walter Gropius. They had taught at the Bauhaus in Germany. (The Bauhaus was a school that trained architects and designers who made things that were mass-produced. Bauhaus artists created simple, geometric forms without ornament, and they preferred primary colors or black and white.)

The Bauhaus influence is evident in the Executive electric typewriter Noyes designed for IBM in 1959 (Fig. 5.7). Its smooth, rounded form brought a new sculptural quality to office equipment. And the color choices included red, yellow, and blue. Noyes revolutionized the electric typewriter again when he designed the IBM Selectric two years later. For this machine he introduced a type ball, the size of a golf ball, with all the letters and numbers

Fig. 5.6. Valentine I-47 typewriter, designed by Ettore Sottsass Jr. for Olivetti, 1969

Fig. 5.7. IBM Executive
electric typewriter, 1959

on it instead of on individual type bars. The ball moved while the paper stayed still, eliminating the need for a carriage. Typing had become quieter, easier, and faster.

Actually, this single-element idea for electric typewriters had been explored years earlier, in 1902, by Blickensderfer. Blickensderfer was also a pioneer in adapting electricity to typewriters and produced the Thick Electric. James Smathers, an industrial engineer, patented the idea behind most modern electric typewriters during the World War I period. IBM began selling its first electric typewriter based on Smathers's idea in 1931, but it wasn't until the 1950s that electric typewriters became widely used.

The arrival of computers for business and personal use in the 1970s caused the near death of the typewriter. (But those who love typewriters still have them and enjoy them.) Only one part of the typewriter carried over to the computer—the QWERTY keyboard.

Despite advances in technology and inventions such as the typewriter and computer, many people still have pencils on their desks. When they begin to write something, they pick up a pencil.

Certain forms of computer software use a pencil and eraser as an icon. Click on the icon, and the most recent entry is deleted. According to the Joseph Dixon Ticonderoga Company, "There will always be a pencil."

6 . . . .

Does It Suit
Your Fancy?

CHIME

When Henry Dreyfuss was asked how he started solving an industrial design problem, he said he *began* with men, women, and children, and *ended* with them. He considered the habits of the people who would use the item—their size, and their likes and dislikes. When he was asked to redesign an alarm clock that wasn't selling well, he toured the clock counters in many New York stores. Dreyfuss noticed people squinting at the face of his client's clock and fumbling with the winders on the back. Then he watched customers weigh the clocks in their hands and pick the ones that were heavier than his. Did they think that a heavier clock was a better one?

Next he took the clock home to check it out for himself. Who would use it? he wondered. He asked various people of different shapes and sizes to wind it, until he created a winder that fit most fingers. Then, with sketches and models, he began redesigning the face of the clock. The numbers had to be easy to read, especially first thing in the morning. To test out the faces, he lined up ten clocks by his bedside every night, with the alarms set for various times, starting at 4:00 A.M. This may have irritated his wife, but because she loved him and was his business partner, she went along with his project. Finally, through trial and error, Dreyfuss designed just the right clock face. He added a heavy base to the clock to give it the weight people seemed to prefer. And he brightened the appearance with fresh colors. In a few months his new clock went on the market—and soon became a best-seller.

What new products will the future bring? How will everyday objects change? Industrial designers often redesign things that don't work properly, or they invent new products to make tasks easier, more comfortable, and efficient. What things around your house need improvement? If you were to pick one thing that might benefit from being redesigned, how would you start?

Dreyfuss suggested this exercise to those interested in industrial design: "Just look around your own home. Select a dozen items that do not suit your fancy and seriously study them, then make an attempt to redesign them."

First you would have to study the thing and see how it works—or doesn't. What task is it supposed to do? Does it do it? If not, why? What's the problem? How could this thing work better? Is it simple to use or too complicated? Is it safe? Easy to fix? Easy to clean? Who uses it? Where? When? Is it the right size and shape? Does it have pleasing form and color? What's it made of, anyway? Could it be made of something else? Is such a material available?

How will you know if your new design is good? Dreyfuss said, "If . . . people are made safer, more comfortable . . . more efficient—or just plain happier [by contact with the product]— the designer has succeeded."

Afterword

I discovered the wonderful world of applied arts when I was twelve. Growing up in the Bronx, I had shared a small bathroom with my parents and older brother. It was hard to get in there, and once I did, it was nothing special. The toilet, sink, and combination bathtub/shower were, of course, white. So was the plastic shower curtain. It didn't occur to me that bathroom fixtures could ever come in any other color until I visited some new friends of my parents who lived in suburban New Jersey.

Their daughter was my age and she showed me around the house. What impressed me most was her bathroom. It was all pink—toilet, sink, and tub! What's more, there was a separate stall shower with a glass door. Using the pink bathroom that weekend made me feel like a different person. Elegant. Pampered. I realized bathrooms could be beautiful. I started looking at everything around me, deciding what I liked and what I didn't like—and questioning why.

As a young art student in New York, I often went to the Museum of Modern Art. While I enjoyed the paintings, drawings, and sculptures, I was amazed to stumble upon an area upstairs devoted to the decorative arts. There, behind glass cases, were ordinary things—telephones, typewriters, toasters. They were displayed as works of art and I responded to them. They had pleasing lines, shapes, and colors. Without knowing it, I was learning about good design.

As an adult, I have often thought of the exhibits I saw in the Department of Architecture and Design at the Museum of Modern Art. I recently had to buy a stove when we remodeled our kitchen. What won me over was a stove with red knobs, just as pink bathroom fixtures had dazzled me years ago. This was the beginning of *Toilets, Toasters & Telephones: The How and Why of Everyday Objects*.

Acknowledgments

Chapter 1. A Bathroom Is a Bathroom

Chapter opener, p. 1. Ponti toilet (detail). Photo courtesy of the Philadelphia Museum of Art. Gift of Ideal Standard

Fig. 1.2, p. 4. Photo courtesy of The Egypt Exploration Society

Fig. 1.3, p. 7. Photo courtesy of Moorlands Photolabs Ltd., Armitage Shanks, Ltd., manufacturer

Fig. 1.4, p. 13. Photo courtesy of the Philadelphia Museum of Art. Gift of Ideal Standard

Fig. 1.6, p. 17. Photo courtesy of the Museum of Modern Art, New York, and American Standard

Fig. 1.8, p. 22. Engraving courtesy of Cooper-Hewitt, National Design Museum, Smithsonian Institution/Art Resource, NY. Gift of Mrs. Leo Wallerstein, *1962-181-1.* Photo by Matt Flynn

Fig. 1.9, p. 25. Photo courtesy of Warshaw Collection of Business Americana, Archives Center, National Museum of American History, Smithsonian Institution

Poetry extract, p. 26. "Splash" by Ogden Nash. From VERSES FROM 1929 ON by Ogden Nash. Copyright 1935 by Ogden Nash; first appeared in *The Saturday Evening Post.* By permission of Little, Brown and Company. Reprinted by permission of Curtis Brown, Ltd. Copyright © 1938, renewed by the Estate of Ogden Nash

Chapter 2. What's Cooking?

Chapter opener, p. 29. Automatic electric toaster, circa 1965. Photo courtesy of Science Museum, Science & Society Picture Library, London

Fig. 2.2, p. 32. Drawing courtesy of Museum of Welsh Life (National Museums & Galleries of Wales)

Fig. 2.3, p. 36. Photo courtesy of the Norman Bel Geddes Collection/The Theatre Arts Collection, Harry Ransom Humanities Research Center, the University of Texas at Austin. By permission of Edith Lutyens Bel Geddes, Executrix

Fig. 2.5, p. 43. Photo by Jeffrey Milstein for Paper House Productions—note cards, magnets, and stickers

Chapter 3. Cleaning Up

Chapter opener, p. 53. Photo courtesy of the Hoover Co., North Canton, Ohio

Fig. 3.2, p. 56. From *California Lettersheets #43*—"Sundry Amusements in the Mines." Reproduced by permission of The Huntington Library, San Marino, California

Fig. 3.3, p. 59. Illustration from *American Design Ethic* by Arthur J. Pulos, Cambridge, Massachusetts: The MIT Press, 1986. Used by permission

Figs. 3.5, 3.6, pp. 64, 65. Photos courtesy of Science & Society Picture Library/Science Museum, London

Fig. 3.7, p. 66. Photo courtesy of Cooper-Hewitt, National Design Museum, Smithsonian Institution/Art Resource, NY

Figs. 3.9, 3.10, 3.11, 3.12, pp. 70, 71, 72, 74. Photos courtesy of the Hoover Co., North Canton, Ohio

Chapter 4. "Hello! Are You There?"

Chapter opener, p. 77. Model 302 telephone, 1937 (detail). Photo courtesy of Bell Telephone Laboratories, Henry Dreyfuss Collection, Cooper-Hewitt, National Design Museum, Smithsonian Institution/Art Resource, NY

Figs. 4.2, 4.3, 4.4, pp. 81, 82, 83. Photos property of AT&T Archives. Reprinted with permission of AT&T

Fig. 4.5, p. 85. Photo by Jeffrey Milstein for Paper House Productions—note cards, magnets, and stickers

Figs. 4.6, 4.7, pp. 86, 88. Photos courtesy of Bell Telephone Laboratories, Henry Dreyfuss Collection, Cooper-Hewitt, National Design Museum, Smithsonian Institution/Art Resource, NY

Chapter 5. QWERTY?

Chapter opener, p. 91. Underwood typewriter (detail). Photo courtesy of Science & Society Picture Library/Science Museum, London

Figs. 5.2, 5.3, pp. 95, 96. Photos courtesy of the Gillette Company

Fig. 5.5, p. 105. Photo courtesy of Science & Society Picture Library/Science Museum, London

Figs. 5.6, 5.7, pp. 107, 108. Photos courtesy of Denver Art Museum, museum purchase with funds from the Ice House Benefit Fund, 1989

Chapter 6. Does It Suit Your Fancy?

Chapter opener, p. 111. Alarm clock, 1939 (detail). Designed by Henry Dreyfuss, 1904–1972. Made by Western Clock Co. (Westclox), LaSalle, Illinois. Courtesy of Henry Dreyfuss Collection, Cooper-Hewitt, National Design Museum, Smithsonian Institution/Art Resource, NY. Gift of Henry Dreyfuss, 1972-88-283.1

Bibliography

Books

Adler, Michael H. *The Writing Machine: A History of the Typewriter.* London: George Allen & Unwin Ltd., 1973.

Ahern, Eleanor. *The Way We Wash Our Clothes.* New York: M. Barros & Company, 1941 (special Procter & Gamble edition).

* Allaback, Steven. "Henry Wadsworth Longfellow." *Dictionary of Literary Biography.* Vol. 1, *The American Rennaissance in New England.* Edited by Joel Myerson. Detroit: Gale Research Company, 1978.

* Editors of American Heritage. *The California Gold Rush.* Narrative by Ralph A. Andrist. New York: American Heritage Publishing Co., Inc., 1961.

* Ardley, Neil. *Computers.* New York: Warwick Press, 1983.

* Artman, E. Townsend. *Toasters 1909–1960.* Atglen, Pa.: Schiffer Publishing Ltd.,1996.

Bel Geddes, Norman. *Horizons.* Boston: Little, Brown and Company, 1932.

Bush, Donald J. *The Streamlined Decade.* New York: George Braziller, 1975.

Chermayeff, Serge, and Rene D'Harnoncourt. "Design for Use." *Art in Progress: A Survey for the Fifteenth Anniversary of the Museum of Modern Art.* New York: Museum of Modern Art, 1944.

* Choron, Sandra. *The Big Book of Kids' Lists.* New York: World Almanac Publications, 1985.

* *Books suitable for young readers*

121

* Colman, Penny. *Toilets, Bathtubs, Sinks, and Sewers: A History of the Bathroom.* New York: Atheneum, 1994.

Conran, Terence. *The Kitchen Book.* New York: Crown Publishers, 1977.

* Darling, David J. *Inside Computers: Hardware and Software.* Minneapolis: Dillon Press 1986.

* Davidson, Caroline. *A Woman's Work Is Never Done: A History of Housework in the British Isles 1650–1950.* London: Chatto & Windus, 1982.

* Dreyfuss, Henry. *Designing for People.* New York: Simon and Schuster, 1955.

Flinchum, Russell. *Henry Dreyfuss, Industrial Designer: The Man in the Brown Suit.* New York: Cooper-Hewitt National Design Museum, Smithsonian Institution, and Rizzoli, 1997.

* Fortis, Alex, and Antonio Vannucchi. *Fountain Pens.* San Francisco: Chronicle Books, 1995.

Franklin, Linda Campbell. *300 Years of Kitchen Collectibles: A Price Guide for Collectors.* Florence, Ala.: Books Americana, Inc., 1981.

Furnas, J. C. *The Americans: A Social History of the United States, 1587–1914.* New York: G. P. Putnam's Sons, 1969.

Garrett, Elisabeth Donaghy. *At Home: The American Family 1750–1870.* New York: Harry N. Abrams, 1990.

* Giblin, James Cross. *Be Seated: A Book about Chairs.* New York: HarperCollins Publishers, 1993.

Habeeb, Virginia T. *Thousands of Creative Kitchen Ideas.* New York: Funk & Wagnalls, 1976.

* Harrison, Mollie. *The Kitchen in History.* New York: Charles Scribner's Sons, 1972.

Hiesinger, Kathryn B., and George H. Marcus, editors. *Design Since 1945.* Philadelphia: Philadelphia Museum of Art, 1983

———. *Landmarks of Twentieth-Century Design.* New York: Abbeville Press, 1993.

* Hoobler, Dorothy, and Thomas Hoobler. *The Chinese American Family Album.* New York: Oxford University Press, 1994.

* Howarth, Sarah. *Medieval Places.* Brookfield, Conn.: Millbrook Press, 1992.

James, Simon. *Ancient Rome.* New York: Knopf, 1990.

* Jones, Charlotte Foltz. *Mistakes That Worked.* New York: Doubleday, 1981.

* Kira, Alexander. *The Bathroom. Criteria for Design.* Ithaca, N.Y.: Cornell University Press, 1966.

La Pietra, Ugo, editor. *Gio Ponti.* New York: Rizzoli, 1996.

Leffingwell, Randy. *John Deere Farm Tractors: A History of the John Deere Tractor.* Osceola, Wis.: Motorbooks International, 1993.

Loewy, Raymond. *Never Leave Well Enough Alone.* New York: Simon and Schuster, 1951.

Lupton, Ellen. *Mechanical Brides.* New York: Cooper-Hewitt National Design Museum, Smithsonian Institution, and Princeton Architectural Press, 1993.

Meikle, Jeffrey K. *Twentieth Century Limited.* Philadelphia: Temple University Press, 1979.

* Meltzer, Milton. *Mark Twain: A Writer's Life.* New York: Franklin Watts, 1985.

Myerson, Jeremy, and Sylvia Katz. *Home Office.* New York: Van Nostrand Reinhold, 1990.

————. *Kitchenware.* New York: Van Nostrand Reinhold, 1990.

* Nash, Ogden. *I'm a Stranger Here Myself.* Boston: Little, Brown and Company, 1938.

Norman, Donald A. *The Psychology of Everyday Things.* New York: Basic Books, Inc., 1988.

Palmer, Roy. *The Water Closet: A New History.* Newton Abbot, England: David & Charles, 1973.

* Parker, Steve. *53½ Things That Changed the World and Some That Didn't!* Brookfield, Conn.: Millbrook Press, 1992.

Petrowski, Henry. *The Pencil.* New York: Alfred A. Knopf, 1990.

Pile, John. *The Dictionary of 20th-Century Design.* New York: Da Capo Press, 1994.

* Polley, Jane, editor. *Stories Behind Everyday Things.* Pleasantville, N.Y.: The Reader's Digest Association, 1980.

Potter, T. W. *Roman Italy.* Berkeley: University of California Press, 1987.

* Pudney, John. *The Smallest Room.* London: Michael Joseph Ltd., 1959.

Pulos, Arthur J. *American Design Ethic.* Cambridge, Mass.: MIT Press, 1986.

————. *The American Design Adventure, 1940–1975.* Cambridge, Mass: MIT Press, 1990.

Reid, Donald. *Paris Sewers and Sewer Men.* Cambridge, Mass: Harvard University Press, 1991.

* Reyburn, Wallace. *Flushed with Pride: The Story of Thomas Crapper.* London: Macdonald and Company, 1969.

Reynolds, Reginald. *Cleanliness and Godliness.* New York: Doubleday and Company, Inc., 1946.

Riley, Terence, and Edward Eigen. "Between the Museum and the Marketplace: Selling Good Design." *The Museum of Modern Art at Mid-Century.* New York: Harry N. Abrams, Inc., 1994.

Roberts, William, Esq. *History of Letter-Writing.* London: William Pickering, 1843.

* Rubio, Mary, and Elizabeth Waterston, editors. *The Selected Journals of L. M. Montgomery.* Vol. 1: 1889–1910. Toronto: Oxford University Press, 1985.

Saintsbury, George. *A Letter Book: Selected with an Introduction on the History and Art of Letter-Writing.* London: G. Bell and Sons, Ltd.; New York: Harcourt Brace & Company, 1922.

* Schneiderman, Ron. *Computers: From Babbage to the Fifth Generation.* New York: Franklin Watts, 1986.

See, Lisa. *On Gold Mountain.* New York: St. Martin's Press, 1995.

* Severn, Bill. *William Howard Taft: The President Who Became Chief Justice.* New York: David McKay Company, Inc., 1970.

Sparke, Penny. *An Introduction to Design and Culture in the Twentieth Century.* New York: Harper & Row, Publishers, 1986.

* Stern, Ellen, and Emily Gwathmey. *Once Upon a Telephone.* New York: Harcourt Brace & Company, 1994.

Strasser, Susan. *Never Done: A History of American Housework.* New York: Pantheon Books, 1982.

* Sturtevant, William C., editor. *Handbook of North American Indians.* No. 8 (California). Washington, D.C.: Smithsonian Institution, 1978–1996.

* Sutton, Caroline, with Duncan M. Anderson. *How Do They Do That? Wonders of the Modern World Explained.* New York: William Morrow and Company, Inc., 1981.

Van Doren, Harold. *Industrial Design.* New York: McGraw-Hill Book Company, Inc., 1940.

Wishart, John, editor. *Selected English Letters.* New York: E. P. Dutton and Company.

Wright, Lawrence. *Clean and Decent: The Fascinating History of the Bathroom and Water Closet.* London: Routledge & Kegan Paul, 1960.

Periodicals and Newspapers

Burdick, Alan. "What I've Learned from Toast." *The New York Times Magazine* (March 10, 1996), 78.

Davidson, Bill. "You Buy Their Dreams." *Collier's* 120 (August 2, 1947), 23.

Dreyfuss, Henry. "Adapting Products to People," *Bell Telephone Magazine* 46 (September/October 1967), 23.

———. "The Industrial Designer—His Role and Purpose." *Bell Laboratories Record* 40, no. 9 (October 1962), 332–35.

———. "The Profile of Industrial Design." *Machine Design* (June 22, 1967), 2–7.

———. "Designing the Product to Suit Human Dimensions." *Engineering Magazine* (September 1955).

Guilfoyle, J. Roger, editor-in-chief. "Doris and Henry." *Industrial Design* (October 1972), 23.

Hendrick, Kimmis. "Questions Trigger the Flash." *Christian Science Monitor,* May 11–13, 1968 (weekend issue).

Huneven, Michelle. "Eat or Be Eaten." *The New York Times Magazine* (March 10, 1996), 62.

Johnston, Alva. "Nothing Looks Right to Dreyfuss." *Saturday Evening Post* (November 22, 1947), 20–21, 132–39.

Kleinfield, N. R. "Industrial Design Comes of Age." *New York Times,* March 10, 1985.

Stovall, Margaret. "Product Designer Dreyfuss Created Familiar Phone Shape." *Independent Star-News* (Pasadena, Calif.), July 20, 1968.

"Both Fish and Fowl." *Fortune* 9 (February 1934), 40–43, 88–90, 97–98.

"Henry Dreyfuss 1904–1972." *Industrial Design* 20, no. 2 (March, 1973), 37–43.

"Industry Warms Up to Microwaves." *Business Week* (March 11, 1965), 152, 154, 156.

"Management: Art for Profit's Sake." *Investor's Reader* (November 3, 1952), 10–13.

Other Publications

Denenberg, Thomas. "The Longfellows at Craigie House." *A Historic Resource Study: Historical Overview and Evaluation of Significance,* Part 2. Cambridge, Mass.: Longfellow National Historic Site, 1996.

Vagos, Marc. *A Plumbing History of Craigie House.* Cambridge, Mass.: Longfellow National Historic Site, 1978.

Exhibits, Catalogs, and Lectures

Dreyfuss, Henry. "Welcome to My Dream House." Lecture. McCall's Congress on Better Living. Washington, D.C.: October 7, 1958.

Henry Dreyfuss Archive. New York: Cooper-Hewitt National Design Museum.

Hose, Robert H. (partner of Henry Dreyfuss). Dinner address, Park Sheraton. General Electric Advanced Marketing Management Seminar. New York: May 27, 1953.

Johnson, Philip. *Machine Art.* Exhibition catalog. Foreword by Alfred H. Barr. New York: The Museum of Modern Art, 1934.

Lupton, Ellen, and J. Abbott Miller. *The Bathroom, the Kitchen and the Aesthetics of Waste: A Process of Elimination.* Cambridge, Mass.: MIT List Visual Arts Center, 1992.

Index